HOTEL MANAGEMENT
Marketing, Sales and Accounting

HOTEL MANAGEMENT

Marketing, Sales and Accounting

MRIDULA MIRAJKAR

KANISHKA PUBLISHERS, DISTRIBUTORS
NEW DELHI-110 002

KANISHKA PUBLISHERS, DISTRIBUTORS
4697/5-21A, Ansari Road, Daryaganj
New Delhi-110 002
Phones : 2327 0497, 2328 8285
Fax : 011-2328 8285
e-mail: kanishka_publishing@yahoo.co.in

First Published 2008

ISBN 978-81-8457-093-9

PRINTED IN INDIA

Published by Madan Sachdeva for Kanishka Publishers, Distributors, 4697/5-21A, Ansari Road, Daryaganj, New Delhi-110 002; Typeset by Sunshine Graphics, Delhi, and Printed at Nice Printing Press, Delhi.

Preface

Hotel Management: Marketing, Sales and Accounting provides an insight into the issues related to marketing, sales, accounting and management of hotel industries operating across the world. An introduction to hotel and lodging industries is provided with elaborate focus on hotels, motels, resorts, tourist resorts, apartments, suites, guest houses, hostels, etc. An overview of various typologies of lodging facilities is provided with focus on bed and breakfast. Major issues and areas related to hotel and hospitality services management are covered in detail with special focus on guest revenue in resort hotels.

Case studies of select few service management companies in the related areas are presented. An overview of access hotel management is also provided herein. The book also imparts knowledge about hotel marketing, sales and consulting, with particular focus on training aspects. Relevant select case studies are done to further illustrate the issues in questions and the options available. Focus also lies on aspects related to software development and ID Badges applicable in hotel accounting services. Most of the accounting softwares being used in sales and marketing are covered, with detailed practices undertaken by select hotel services industries across the world. Similarly, the uses of ID Badges in restaurant/hospitality accounting have been outlined, with focus on select case studies.

This book also addresses issues related to role of hotel manager, motel manager and resort manager. Case studies of select companies are provided in brief. An overview of hotel manages, sales, and marketing services and hotel/resort software is given. Relevant case studies and guidelines are dealt in detail. An outline of hotel management technology course is also provided. The book boosts of including important appendices related to worldwide listing of accounting/finance/tax-related websites and individualized studies. A detailed bibliography is provided to facilitate further research and study.

MRIDULA MIRAJKAR

Contents

Chapter 1

Introduction to Hotel and Lodging Industry

HOTEL

A hotel is an establishment that provides paid lodging, usually on a short-term basis. Hotels often provide a number of additional guest services such as a restaurant, a swimming pool or childcare. Some hotels have conference services and meeting rooms and encourage groups to hold conventions and meetings at their location. Hotels differ from motels in that most motels have drive-up, exterior entrances to the rooms, while hotels tend to have interior entrances to the rooms, which may increase guests' safety and present a more upmarket image.

In Australia, a hotel may also be an establishment that serves alcoholic drinks, and usually meals in a casual setting but which does not necessarily provide accommodation. This type of establishment would more usually be called a pub or bar in other countries. In general use in Australia the terms '"hotel" and *pub* are usually taken to be synonymous.

Origins of the Term

The word *hotel* derives from the French *hôtel,* which referred to a French version of a townhouse or any other building seeing frequent visitors, not a place offering accommodation (in contemporary usage, *hôtel* has the meaning of "hotel", and *hôtel particulier* is used for the old meaning). The French spelling (with the circumflex) was once also used in English, but is now rare. The circumflex replaces the 's' once preceding the 't' in the earlier *hostel* spelling, which over time received a new, but closely related meaning.

Services and Facilities

Basic accommodation of a room with only a bed, a cupboard, a small table and a washstand has largely been replaced by rooms with en-suite bathrooms and climate control. Other features found may be a telephone, an alarm clock, a TV, and broadband Internet connectivity. Food and drink may be supplied by a mini-bar (which often includes a small refrigerator) containing snacks and drinks (to be paid for on departure), and tea and coffee making facilities (cups, spoons, an electric kettle and sachets containing instant coffee, tea bags, sugar, and creamer or milk).

Some hotels offer various combinations of meals as part of a room and board arrangement. These are often advertised as:

European Plan — no meals are included, or only a minimal breakfast.
American Plan — all meals included (full board).
Modified American Plan option of breakfasts and dinners.

In the United Kingdom a hotel is required by law to serve food and drinks to all comers within certain stated hours; to avoid this requirement it is not uncommon to come across "private hotels" which are not subject to this requirement.

However, in Japan the capsule hotel supplies minimal facilities and room space.

Classification

The cost and quality of hotels are usually indicative of the range and type of services available. Due to the enormous increase in tourism worldwide during the last decades of the 20th century, standards, especially those of smaller establishments, have improved considerably. For the sake of greater comparability, rating systems have been introduced, with the one to five stars classification being most common.

Boutique Hotels

"Boutique Hotel" is a term originating in North America to describe intimate, usually luxurious or quirky hotel environments. Boutique hotels differentiate themselves from larger chain or branded hotels by providing an exceptional and personalized level of accommodation, services and facilities. Because of their financial successes in the most recent past, there have been attempts to create chains have adopted the "boutique" look and feel. In the US this trend was started by the "W" hotel chain in the 1990s and most recently this trend can be observed in chains as "aloft", "NYLO", "Hyatt Place" and others. Through this corporate adaptation of the concept the term "boutique" also changed and more recently hoteliers prefer to use the term "lifestyle hotels" to get away from the above mentioned quirky image.

Boutique hotels are sometimes furnished in a themed, stylish and/or aspirational manner. Although usually considerably smaller than a mainstream hotel (ranging from 3 to 100 guest rooms) boutique hotels are generally fitted with telephone and wi-fi Internet connections, honesty bars and often cable/pay TV. Guest services are attended to by 24 hours hotel staff. Many of the boutique hotels have on site dining facilities, and the majority offer attractive bars as well as lounges which may also be open to the general public. Of the total travel market a small percentage are discerning travellers, who place a high importance on privacy, luxury and service delivery. This market is typically price insensitive (made up of both high end leisure and corporate travellers), non-seasonal, high-yielding and repeat, and therefore one which boutique hotel and other high-end operators target as their primary source of income.

Motels

There is no hard and fast rule differentiating motels from other hotels, although the word *motel* suggests that it is aimed at motorists. This may simply mean that it is a hotel with good access to the road network (on a motorway or ring road) so that a long car journey need not be interrupted for long by town-centre traffic. In other cases the designation is simply an attempt to make the most of a poor location inconvenient for town-centre services and attractions. Classically, though, a *motel* is a hotel which is made convenient for people who, for whatever personal reason, wish to be able to have quick access from the outside world (especially from their parked car) to the hotel room—without passing the scrutiny of a receptionist or fellow guests. This is usually arranged by having rooms (sometimes in individual chalets or even trailers) arranged around the car park with room doors opening directly to the outside rather than to an internal corridor.

Historic Hotels

Some hotels have gained their renown through tradition, by hosting significant events or persons, such as Schloss *Cecilienhof* in Potsdam, Germany, which derives its fame from the so-called Potsdam Conference of the World War II allies Winston Churchill, Harry Truman and Joseph Stalin in 1945. The Taj Mahal Palace & Tower in Mumbai is one India's most famous and historic hotels because of its association with the Indian independence movement. Other establishments have given name to a particular meal or beverage, as is the case with the *Waldorf Astoria* in New York City, USA, known for its *Waldorf Salad* or the *Raffles Hotel* in Singapore, where the drink *Singapore Sling* was invented. Another example is the *Hotel Sacher* in Vienna Austria, home of the *Sachertorte*, or even the Hotel de Paris where the crepe Suzette was invented. There are also hotels which became much more popular through films like the *Grand Hotel Europe* in Saint Petersburg, Russia when James Bond stayed there in the Blockbuster, Goldeneye. Cannes hotels such as the *Carlton* or the *Martinez* become the centre of the world during Cannes Film Festival (France).

A number of hotels have entered the public consciousness through popular culture, such as the *Ritz Hotel* in London, UK ('Putting on The Ritz'). The Algonquin Hotel in New York City with its famed Algonquin Round Table and Hotel Chelsea, also in New York City, subject of a number of songs and also the scene of the stabbing of Nancy Spungen (allegedly by her boyfriend Sid Vicious). Hotels that enter folklore like these two are also often frequented by celebrities, as is the case both with the Ritz and the Chelsea.

Unusual Hotels

Many hotels can be considered destinations in themselves, by dint of unusual features of the lodging and/or its immediate environment:

Treehouse Hotels

Some hotels, such as the Costa Rica Tree House in the Gandoca-Manzanillo Wildlife Refuge, Costa Rica, or Treetops Hotel in Aberdare National Park, Kenya, are built with living trees as structural elements, making them treehouses. The Ariau Towers near Manaus, Brazil is in the middle of the Amazon, on the Rio Negro. Bill Gates even invested and had a suite built there with satellite internet/phone.

Another hotel with treehouse units is Bayram's Tree Houses in Olympos, Turkey. Another ecological treehouse hotel is in the natural reserve at Rio Claro, Antioquia, (Colombia).

Cave Hotels

Desert Cave Hotel in Coober Pedy, South Australia and the Cuevas Pedro Antonio de Alarcón (named after the author) in Guadix, Spain, as well as several hotels in Cappadocia, Turkey, are notable for being built into natural cave formations, some with rooms underground.

Capsule Hotels

Capsule hotels are a type of economical hotels that are quite common in Japan.

Ice Hotels

Ice hotels, such as the Ice Hotel in Jukkasjärvi, Sweden, melt every spring and are rebuilt out of ice and snow each winter.

Snow Hotels

The Mammut Snow Hotel in Finland is located within the walls of the Kemi snow castle, which is the biggest in the world. It includes *The Mammut Snow Hotel, The Castle Courtyard, The Snow Restaurant* and a chapel for weddings, etc. Its furnishings and decorations, such as sculptures, are all made of snow and ice.

A hotel which offers similar accommodation also in Lainio Snow Hotel in Lapland (near Ylläs), Finland.

Garden Hotels

Garden hotels, famous for their gardens before they became hotels, includes Gravetye Manor, the home of William Robinson and Cliveden, designed by Charles Barry with a rose garden by Geoffrey Jellicoe.

Underwater Hotels

As of 2005, the only hotel with an underwater room that can be reached without Scuba diving is Utter Inn in Lake Mälaren, Sweden. It only has one room, however, and Jules Undersea Lodge in Key Largo, Florida, which requires Scuba diving, is not much bigger. Hydropolis is an ambitious project to build a luxury hotel in Dubai, UAE, with 220 suites, all on the bottom of the Persian Gulf, 20 meters (66 ft.) below the surface. Its architecture will feature two domes that break the surface and an underwater train tunnel, all made of transparent materials such as glass and acrylic.

Other Unusual Hotels

- The Library Hotel in New York City is unique in that its ten floors are arranged according to the *Dewey Decimal System*.
- The *Rogers Centre*, formerly SkyDome, in Toronto, Canada is the only stadium to have a hotel connected to it, with 70 rooms overlooking the field. West Ham United F.C. in the UK now has a hotel with rooms that overlook the pitch and sometimes double as executive boxes for important games, as does Coventry City's Ricoh Arena.
- The Burj al-Arab hotel in Dubai, United Arab Emirates, built on an artificial island, is structured in the shape of a sail of a boat.
- The RMS Queen Mary in Long Beach, California is the only 1930s ocean liner still in existence. Its elegant first-class staterooms are now used as a hotel.

World-Record Setting Hotels

Tallest

The tallest hotel in the world is thought to be the Burj al-Arab in Dubai, United Arab Emirates at 321 meters (1,053 feet). However, this title may be taken by the less illustrious Ryugyong Hotel in Pyongyang at 330 meters (1,083 feet), pending its (perhaps unlikely) completion; it has been under construction since 1987 and was abandoned in 1992.

Largest

The current largest hotel in the world is First World Hotel in Genting Highlands, Malaysia. It has a total of 6,118 rooms, and is part of the Genting Highlands Resort and Casino. The First World Plaza which is adjoined to the two hotel towers boasts 500,000 square feet of indoor theme park, shopping centres, casino gaming areas, and eateries. Previously, the largest hotel in the world was the MGM Grand Las Vegas in Las Vegas, Nevada, USA with 5,690 rooms.

Oldest

According to the Guinness Book of World Records, the oldest hotel still in operation is the Hoshi Ryokan, in Awazu, Japan. It opened in 717 CE, and features hot springs.

Hotel Occupations

The owner, Chairman, or CEO of a hotel or hotel group is known as a *hotelier*. The front desk, reservations, housekeeping, security, or loss prevention, valet parking, transportation, uniformed services (which may refer to bellmen, doormen, and even concierge) food and beverage, accounting, sales, marketing, catering, audio visual, and engineering or maintenance are common departments of a mid or large sized hotel. The night auditor role falls within the front desk department but also carries some of the responsibilities of the accounting department. The engineering staff takes care of building repairs and up keep of HVAC systems, plumbing, fire sprinkler systems, chillers, cooling towers, pool and spa if applicable, lights, breakers, door locks, C.P.R., laundry machines, kitchen walk ins, ice machines, building air handlers, room repairs and upkeep.

Hotel Chains

A hotel chain is a collection or grouping of hotels under one recognizable brand operated by a management company. Best Western International claims to be the largest hotel chain in the world, in terms of the number of properties.

Living in Hotels

The American billionaire Howard Hughes lived much of his life in hotels. He moved with his entourage from hotel to hotel and from Beverly Hills to Boston before deciding to move to Las Vegas and become a casino baron. Less than a month after his November 27, 1966 arrival, Hughes made a public offer to buy the Desert Inn. The hotel's 8th floor became the nerve centre of his empire and the 9th floor penthouse became Hughes' personal residence. Hughes moved to the Bahamas, Vancouver, London and several other locations—always taking up residence in the top floor penthouse of the hotel. Between 1966 and 1968, he also purchased several other hotel-casinos from the Mafia: Castaways, New Frontier, The Landmark Hotel and Casino, Sands and Silver Slipper.

Coco Chanel made the Hôtel Ritz in Paris her home for more than thirty years, until the day of her death, at 87, in a suite now named "Coco Chanel Suite".

King Peter II of Yugoslavia spent much of the Second World War at Claridge's, a hotel in London. His son, Aleksandar Karađorđević, was born in the hotel.

Prince Felix Yusupov lived in the Hotel Vendôme in Paris.

Alois Brunner, Austrian Nazi war criminal, is believed to have lived in the Meridian Hotel in Damascus, Syria, under the name Georg Fischer.

Sultan Said Bin Taimur of Muscat lived at Dorchester Hotel in London after he was deposed by Qaboos of Oman in 1970. He died in the hotel in 1972.

Eleftherios Venizelos, Greek statesman and diplomat, lived in the Hôtel Ritz Paris while he was in exile in France from 1935-1936.

Actress Elaine Stritch lives at the Carlyle Hotel in New York City.

Magician Criss Angel lives at the Luxor Hotel in Las Vegas, Nevada. As of late 2006 - present in the Presidential suite.

MOTEL

Entering dictionaries after World War II, the word *motel* (from MOtorists' hoTEL) referred initially to a single building of connected rooms whose doors face a parking lot and/or common area or a series of small cabins with common parking. Their creation was driven by increased driving distances on the United States highway system that allowed easy cross-country travel. The concept originated with the Motel Inn of San Luis Obispo, constructed in 1925 by Arthur Heinman.

Unlike their predecessors, auto camps and tourist courts, motels quickly adopted a homogenized appearance. Typically one would find an 'I' or 'L' or 'U' shaped structure that included rooms, an attached manager's office, and perhaps a small diner. Postwar motels sought more visual distinction, often featuring eye-catching neon signs which employed pop culture themes that ranged from Western imagery of cowboys and Indians to contemporary images of spaceships and atomic symbols.

The motel began in the 1920s as mom-and-pop motor courts on the outskirts of a town. They attracted the first road warriors as they crossed the U.S. in their new automobiles. They usually had a grouping of small cabins and their anonymity made them ideal trysting places (or the "hot trade" in industry lingo). Even the famous outlaws Bonnie and Clyde were frequent guests, using motels as hideouts. The motels' potential for breeding lust and larceny alarmed then FBI Chief J. Edgar Hoover, who attacked motels and auto camps in an article he penned called "Camps of Crime", which ran in the February 1940 issue of American Magazine.

Motels differed from hotels in their emphasis on largely anonymous interactions between owners and occupants, their location along highways (as opposed to urban cores), and their orientation to the outside (in contrast to hotels whose doors typically face an interior hallway).

With the 1952 introduction of Kemmons Wilson's Holiday Inn, the 'mom and pop' motels of that era went into decline. Eventually, the emergence of the interstate highway system, along with other factors, led to a blurring of the motel and the hotel. Today, family owned motels with as few as five rooms may still be found along older highways. The quality and standards of every independent motel differ so it is always wise to cruise around for good motel before settling in a room. In seedy areas, motels also tend to be located near strip clubs. These motels sometimes charge an "hourly" rate instead of a "nightly" rate. Motels with low rates sometimes serve as housing for people who are not able to afford an apartment. The largest budget motel chain is Motel 6.

RESORT

A resort is a place used for relaxation or recreation. As a result, people tend to seek out a resort for holidays or vacations. Generally, a resort is run by a single company, which attempts to provide for all or most of a vacationer's wants while staying there, such as food, drink, lodging, sports, entertainment, and shopping.

Towns that contain resorts—or where tourism or vacationing is a major part of the local activity—are often called resort towns. The term resort is sometimes misused to identify a hotel that does not provide the other amenities required of a resort. However, a hotel is frequently a central feature of a resort.

The Walt Disney World Resort is perhaps the most famous example of a resort in the world, however, resorts exist throughout the world. Resorts are especially prevalent in Central America and the Caribbean.

Types of Resorts

Resort at a Destination

A resort at a destination is a resort that services a destination such as a scenic or historic site, a theme park, a gaming facility or other tourist attraction. Consequently a resort at a destination disputes its guests with other resorts at that destination amongst the public that is attracted by that destination. Examples would be resorts in and around Disney World, resorts in St. Martin in the Caribbean, and resorts at Aspen in the USA.

Destination Resort

A destination resort is a resort that contains, in and of itself, the necessary guest attraction capabilities—that is to say that a destination resort does not need to be near a destination (town, historic site, theme park, or other) to attract its public. Consequently, another characteristic of a destination resort is that is offers food, drink, lodging, sports, entertainment, and shopping within the facility so that guests have no need to leave the facility throughout their stay. Commonly these facilities are of higher quality than would be expected if one were to stay at a hotel or eat in a town's restaurants. Some examples are Atlantis in the Bahamas, Costa do Sauípe in the Northeastern Brazil, Laguna Phuket in Thailand and Sun City near Johannesburg in South Africa.

All-inclusive Resort

An *all-inclusive resort* is a resort that, besides providing all of the common amenities of a resort, charges a fixed price that includes most or all items. At a minimum, most inclusive resorts include lodging, unlimited food, drink, sports activities, and entertainment for the fixed price.

Historical Resorts

The most famous resort of the ancient world was Baiae, Italy, which was popular over 2,000 years ago.

Luxury Resorts

A *luxury resort*, sometimes referred to as an exclusive resort, is a very expensive vacation facility which is fully staffed and has been rated with five stars. *Luxury resorts* often boast many visitor activities and attractions such as golf, watersports, spa and beauty facilities, skiing, natural ecology and tranquility.

A luxury resort is an elite luxury property which exhibits an exceptionally high degree of customer service and hospitality. A flawless execution of guest services will be the resort staff's and managements main concern. A *luxury resort* will commonly also feature a superb architectural interior and exterior design as well as an interesting physical location.

The interior design will normally be elegant with stylish bedroom decor, exceptional dining facilities, and manicured landscaping and meticulous grounds. *Luxury resorts* will often also be in based in exceptionally desirable and strategic worldwide locations, from beautiful tropical islands, to snow caked mountains, to scenic lakes and rivers, to exhilarating cities. The locations will often be famous for featured activities from skiing to golf, water spots, diving, fishing, sailing and nature walks to glamorous shopping and night life entertainment.

A *luxury resort* may vary greatly in character, style and theme from resort to resort. A luxury resort will, however, normally be characterized by a high level of luxury, sophistication and off course price. Accommodations are first class, whether they follow a classic and traditional nature or a more minimalist and modern styling. An unmatched level of comfort will be available at a *luxury resort,* as well as many personalized services and amenities.

Criteria for Resort Development

Physical Infrastructure and Services

Environment

- All environmental laws to be enforced.
- Operators both public and private to comply with environmental regulations.

Security/Safety/Law Enforcement

- Ensure that all laws are enforced with emphasis on municipal laws in respect to parking, solid waste, traffic controls, littering and harassment.
- Ensure that crime is reduced and swift response capabilities are in place to deal with incidents.
- Ramps are put in place to accommodate the disabled.

Safety

- Ensure all public buildings have requisite Fire Safety Certification.

Traffic Flow

- Transport centres should be in place for public transportation.
- Regulated traffic flow systems to be in place and documented.
- Efficient traffic control mechanism to be in place.
- Adequate parking facilities to be in place and regulations adhered to by the public.
- Parking zones to be implemented and enforced.

Pedestrian Zone (Safety)

- Pedestrian zone to be allocated for resort areas.
- Ensure that the resort has adequate space for pedestrians.

Health

All operators require certification from the Ministry of Health:

- There should be strict compliance with Food safety requirements and laws.
- Health facilities must be upto standard in order to service the community.
- Public facilities are to be in good working order.
- There should be adequate health infrastructure for the homeless, mentally ill and indigent.

Sanitation

- Solid waste regulation and laws to be enforced.
- Solid waste collection to be consistent and effectively maintained on a daily, hourly basis.
- Effective maintenance of streets, sidewalks and buildings. All derelict structures to be discarded.
- Drainage to be in good working order.

TOURIST RESORTS: CASE STUDIES

1. Falmouth

Falmouth, considered by many as one of the Caribbean's finest example of a colonial Georgian town, is Jamaica's newest tourist resort. This town was given resort status in September 2005, which is seen as a strategic move in light of major development plans for the parish of Trelawny of which it is capital.

The historical facade of Falmouth with its rustic architecture; beautiful Georgian structures, remnants of the colonial past, and its almost sleepy disposition, makes it an anachronism as it located between two bustling metropolitan resorts, Montego Bay in the west and Ocho Rios in the east. Falmouth is also well-positioned along a major highway connecting the major resort towns, and it is in close proximity to an international airport and a cruise ship pier.

The granting of resort status to Falmouth is timely, as the parish of Trelawny is poised for major multi-million dollar development;—Harmony Cove, a 1000 room upscale hotel expansion, and the new Greenfield Stadium which will host the opening ceremony for Cricket World Cup 2007. The town's development will also fall within TPDCo's heritage development thrust.

These major developments will provide a stimulus for wide-ranging opportunities in the areas of accommodatations, attractions development, entertainment and transportation. Opportunities for employment will also be an added benefit.

2. Portland

Portlanders began this Winter Tourist Season on a high note with the arrival of the first of thirteen cruise ships. Some 13,000 passengers are expected to visit the town during the season, spending in the region of $180 million. The town's people are busy getting their town and its attractions in shape to deal with the influx of visitors over the period, as they begin implementation of a three-year development plan for Portland, spearheaded by TPDCo. Projects to be completed on a phased basis include:

The Beautification of Cenotaph Square

- Painting of buildings in the commercial district.
- The upgrading of facilities at the Musgrave Market for both visitors and locals to patronize local craftspeople and fruit vendors.
- Upgrading of the facilities for rafting on the Rio Grande as well as training and uniform provision for the rafts men.
- Establishment of a Travel Halt at Boston Jerk Centre.
- A Heritage Tour to Folly Ruins.
- A Walking tour of Titchfield Hill.
- Improvements to facilities at Boston Beach and Long Bay Beach.

Appropriate signage at major entrances to the towns, roadways, at attractions and places of interest, and the establishment of information kiosks for visitors, will also form part of the upgrading of the town. Residents are being trained as tour guides and tourism ambassadors.

TPDCo is working to set the tone for improved interaction between the relevant agencies, local authorities and stakeholders in the community to facilitate these improvements, build commitment, and create ownership.

3. South Coast Sustainable Development Programme

A draft project document has been completed for the *South Coast Sustainable Development Programme* and is now awaiting budgetary support for implementation.

The programme aims to meet the economic, social and cultural needs of the people of the South Coast, through a strategy of sustainable and orderly development, in the areas of:

Tourism development and environmental management which respects the unique natural resources of the South Coast, and

Fisheries Management to preserve the biological diversity of the area, and to sustain the social and economic benefits to those communities active in the fisheries sector.

The tourism development plan will span the restoration of Black River to a heritage theme town, community-based tourism development, and the development of a heritage trail in the project area.

The programme which will be implemented over a four-year period is being funded jointly by the Inter-American Development Bank, The Global Environment Facility and the Government of Jamaica.

APARTMENT

An apartment (or *flat* in Britain and most other Commonwealth countries) is a self-contained housing unit that occupies only part of a building. Apartments may be owned (by an *owner-occupier*) or rented (by *tenants*).

Some apartment-dwellers own their apartments, either as co-ops, in which the residents own shares of a corporation that owns the building or development; or in condominiums, whose residents own their apartments and share ownership of the public spaces. Most apartments are in buildings designed for the purpose, but large older houses are sometimes divided into apartments. The word *apartment* connotes a residential unit or section in a building. Apartment building owners, lessors, or managers often use the more general word *units* to refer to apartments. Units can be used to refer to rental business suites as well as residential apartments. When there is no tenant occupying an apartment, the lessor is said to have a *vacancy*. For apartment lessors, each vacancy represents a loss of income from rent-paying tenants for the time the apartment is *vacant* (*i.e.*, unoccupied). Lessors' objectives are often to minimize the vacancy rate for their units. The owner of the apartment typically transfers possession to the occupant(s) by giving him/her the key to the apartment entrance door(s) and any other keys need to live there, such as a common key to the building or any other common areas, and an individual unit mailbox key.

When the occupant(s) move out, these keys should typically be returned to the owner.

Apartment Types and Characteristics

Apartments can be classified into several types. *Studio* or *efficiency* or *bachelor* apartments tend to be the smallest apartments with the cheapest rents in a given area. These kinds of apartment usually consist mainly of a large room which is the living, dining, and bedroom combined. There are usually kitchen facilities as part of this central room, but the bathroom is its own smaller separate room. Moving up from the efficiencies are *one-bedroom apartments* where one bedroom is a separate room from the rest of the apartment. Then there are *two-bedroom, three-bedroom,* etc., apartments. Small apartments often have only one entrance/exit. Large apartments often have two entrances/exits, perhaps a door in the front and another in the back. Depending on the building design, the entrance/exit doors may be directly to the outside or to a common area inside, such as a hallway. Depending on location, apartments may be available for rent *furnished* with furniture or *unfurnished* into which a tenant usually moves in with his/her own furniture. Permanent carpeting is often included in an apartment.

Laundry facilities are usually kept in a separate area accessible to all the tenants in the building. Depending on when the building was built and the design of the building, utilities such as water, heating, and electric may be common for all the apartments in the building or separate for each apartment and billed separately to each tenant (however, many areas in the US have ruled it illegal to split a water bill among all the tenants, especially if a pool is on the premises). Outlets for connection to telephones are typically included in apartments. Telephone service is optional and is practically always billed separately from the rent payments. Cable television and similar amenities are extra also. Parking space(s), air conditioner, and extra storage space may or may not be included with an apartment. Rental leases often limit the maximum number of people who can reside in each apartment. On or around the ground floor of the apartment building, a series of mailboxes are typically kept in a location accessible to the public and, thus, to the letter-carrier too. Every unit typically gets its own mailbox with individual keys to it. Some very large apartment buildings with a full-time staff may take mail from the mailman and provide mail-sorting service. Near the mailboxes or some other location accessible by outsiders, there may be a buzzer (equivalent to a doorbell) for each individual unit. In smaller apartment buildings such as two- or three-flats, or even four-flats, garbage is often disposed of in trash containers similar to those used at houses. In larger buildings, garbage is often collected in a common trash bin or dumpster. For cleanliness or minimizing noise, many lessors will place restrictions on tenants regarding keeping pets in an apartment.

In some parts of the world, the word apartment is used generally to refer to a new purpose-built self-contained residential unit in a building, whereas the word *flat* means a converted self-contained unit in an older building. An industrial, warehouse, or commercial space converted to an apartment is commonly called a loft.

When part of a house is converted for the ostensible use of a landlord's family member, the unit may be known as an *in-law* apartment or *granny flat*, though these (sometimes illegally) created units are often occupied by ordinary renters rather than family members.

Staying in privately owned apartments rather than in a hotel is quickly becoming popular with travellers.

Apartment Hotel

An *Apartment Hotel* (also *ApartHotel*, *Apart Hotel* and *Apart-Hotel*) is a type of accommodation, described as "a serviced apartment complex that uses a hotel style booking system". It is similar to renting an apartment, but with no fixed contracts and occupants can 'check-out' whenever they wish.

Apartment hotels are flexible types of accommodation; instead of the rigid format of a hotel room an apartment hotel complex usually offers a complete fully fitted apartment. These complexes are usually custom built, and similar to a hotel complex contain a varied amount of apartments. The length of stay in these apartment hotel is very varied with anywhere from a few days to months or even years. Prices tend to be cheaper than hotels. The people that stay in apartment hotels use them as a home from home therefore they are usually fitted with everything the average home would require.

Origins

Apartment hotels were first created in holiday destinations as accommodation for families that needed to 'live' in an apartment rather than 'stay' as they would in a hotel. The apartments would provide a 'holiday home' but generally be serviced. Later on these apartments evolved to be complete homes, allowing occupants to do everything they would at home, such as cleaning, washing and cooking.

Services and Facilities

Essentially the apartment hotel combines the flexibility of apartment living with the service of a hotel. Many of the apartments take advantage of prime locations with panoramic views of cities seen through wall to ceiling windows. Suites usually include high quality finishes, broadband connection & interactive TV, servicing and integrated kitchen and bathroom. High quality leather sofas in the living area and king size beds bring the hotel experience to a whole new level. Those are the luxuries, they also come with the basics: satellite or cable TV, washer, dryer, dishwasher, cooker, oven, fridge, freezer, sink, shower, bath, wardrobes, all the furnishings to be expected in a luxury home.

SUITE (HOTEL)

A *suite* in a hotel, mostly denotes a class of luxury rooms. Many large hotels have one or more "honeymoon suites", and sometimes the best room is called the "presidential suite".

Suites offer more space and furniture than a basic hotel room; in addition to the standard bed and bedroom fixtures, a suite will typically add a living room, usually with a couch that folds into a bed. Dining, office and kitchen facilities are also added in some suites. Some hotels now offer only suites. In addition to the luxurious suites mentioned in the first paragraph, regular suites are particularly aimed at travelling businessmen, who would both appreciate additional space and may use it to host small meetings or entertain clients.

Hostal

Hostal is a spanish word for a category of lodging. *Hostales* tend to be somewhat nicer than youth hostels but cheaper than hotels. Accommodations typically include a private bedroom with a sink, and linens are usually provided. Guests may share a common bathroom. Hostales are common in Spain and may also be found in Mexico, Central and South America. They are often family-run and may provide a friendlier and less formal atomsphere than a hotel.

Hostal-residencies are a slightly higher class of accommodation, and are similar to hotels in overall quality.

Extended Stay Hotel

Extended stay hotels are a type of lodging with features unavailable at standard hotels. These features are intended to provide more home-like amenities. There are currently 27 extended stay chains in North America with at least 7 hotels, representing over 2,000 properties. There is substantial variation among extended stay hotels with respect to quality and the amenities that are available. Some of the economy chains attract clientele who use the hotels as semi-permanent lodging. Occasionally, these budget establishments can be the scene of criminal activity.

Extended-stay hotels typically have self-serve laundry facilities and offer discounts for extended stays, beginning at 5 or 7 days. They also have guestrooms (or "suites") with kitchens. The kitchens include at a minimum usually: a sink, a refrigerator (usually full size), a microwave oven, and a stovetop. Some kitchens also have dishwashers and conventional ovens.

Extended stay hotels are popular with business travellers on extended assignments, families in the midst of a relocation, and anyone else in need of temporary housing. Extended stay hotels are also used by travellers who appreciate the larger space a typical suite provides.

History

Residence Inn is credited with popularizing the "extended stay" concept. The chain was launched in 1975 in Wichita, Kansas by Jack DeBoer, and acquired by Marriott Corporation in 1987. As of April 2005, there were over 450 Residence Inn hotels in the United States, Canada and Mexico. Some extended stay hotels are coming up in United Kingdom and Ireland as well.

One of today's most popular long-term lodging brands came from the merger of Extended Stay America and Homestead Hotels. Both these chains were already well-established when they combined in 2004 to become Extended Stay Hotels with over 670 owned and operated properties nationwide.

GUEST HOUSE

A guest house is a private home which has been converted for the exclusive use of guest accommodation. The owner usually lives in an entirely separate area within the property and the guest house may serve as a form of lodging business, similar to a bed and breakfast. Perhaps the most famous example of an individual residing in a guest house was that of Brian "Kato" Kaelin, who was living in such a dwelling on O.J. Simpson's property at the time that Nicole Brown and Ron Goldman were murdered. His presence there led to his later participation as a witness in Simpson's criminal and civil trials.

HOSTEL

Hostels, also called youth hostels, provide short-term accommodation to travellers or backpackers, particularly encouraging outdoor activities and cultural exchange for the young. Hostels are also often called *backpackers' hostels* (or *backpackers'* for short), particularly in Australia and New Zealand.

In a hostel guests often rent a bed (sometimes a bunk bed) in a dormitory and share common bathroom, kitchen, and lounge rooms. Private rooms are often available. The main benefits of a hostel are firstly the low cost of the accommodation compared to alternatives such as hotels, and that one gets to meet other travellers from all over the world. Hostels are usually less formal and less expensive than hotels. They are most frequently used by young travellers. In the past many hostels imposed age limits, but today it is more common for hostels to accept guests of all ages. Despite the openness of modern hostels, the majority of guests are traditionally and overwhelmingly between the ages of 18 and 26.

Hostels provide opportunity for multicultural enlightenment. There is more interaction between guests than in traditional hotels, and many hostels provide activities to their guests for free or at low cost. There are some potential drawbacks to using hostels.

Some hostels have a curfew, daytime lockouts, and/or require occupants to do chores, but often these rules have been abandoned, see below:

Theft can be a problem since guests may share a common living space, but this can be prevented by locking belongings up. Most hostels offer some sort of system for safely storing your valuables, and many offer private lockers. However, for the greater part travellers are equally concerned for the well-being of their own belongings that theft of other people's belongings rarely takes place.

One potential drawback to staying in hostel dormitories is difficulty sleeping because of noise, whether from snoring, someone returning to the room late in the evening, or just general noise from one's living surroundings. For this reason, some hostels associations fix times for last admission and lights out.

Types of Hostels

In 1912 in Altena, Germany, Richard Schirrmann created the first permanent youth hostel. The first hostels were an exponent of the ideology of the German Youth Movement to let (poor) young city people get a fresh breath in the outdoors. The youths were supposed to manage the hostel themselves as much as possible, such as with doing chores (which also kept the costs down).

It was inside Altena castle which had been recently reconstructed. The old rooms are on display now; the youth hostel has moved to new rooms, though it is still inside the castle grounds. These youth hostels now belong to Hostelling International (HI) a nonprofit organisation composed of more than 90 associations representing about 4000 hostels in over 80 countries. Hostelling International was formerly called the International Youth Hostel Federation (IYHF). Since the children were supposed to go out and be active, the hostels were usually closed during the day. At one time HI had tried to limit the use of the terms "hostel" and "youth hostel" to only HI hostels, but today these terms are used for all hostels, whether or not they belong to HI.

In the 1960's and 1970's a new breed of travellers arose, with some shift in motivation, not so much focused on going to the outdoors but to other (often distant) countries to meet new cultures and people, which included other travellers. The hostels were often the best (because cheapest) option to stay the night, but the rules were not in keeping with the new demands. So a new type of hostel arose which did not have curfews, daytime lockouts, or chores. This concept quickly spread all over the world. Most of these newer style hostels do not belong to HI and they often have bars and many of them have very high standards offering twin and double rooms as well as dorms. Since the older style hostels were starting to lose customers they began to adapt, abandoning most of the old rules. Still, alcohol consumption is often not allowed in many hostels, including most HI hostels. Some hostels cater more to school-aged children (sometimes through school trips) and parents with their children, whereas others are more for travellers intent on learning new cultures. Many hostels employ their long-term residents as desk clerks in exchange for free housing.

Similar accommodation can sometimes be found at YMCAs and on school grounds (*e.g.*, campuses) when school is out for summer.

However, while this emphasis on those travelling to explore different cultures and places is emphasised in many hostels, particularly in cities or popular tourist destinations, there are still many hostels providing accommodation for outdoor pursuits such as hillwalking, climbing and bicycle touring. These are often small friendly hostels that retain much of the original vision.

In the UK, 'hostel' also refers to accommodation for homeless people, usually run by Housing Associations or voluntary organisations. Older-style hostels have dormitory style accommodation, newer hostels usually include en-suite accommodation with single-occupancy rooms.

List of Famous Hotel Chains

A hotel chain is a group of branded hotels managed together under a business arrangement known as franchising or operated by a single company.

These include:

- Accor
- Accent inns
- Advena hotels
- AmeriSuites
- AMResorts
- Antara resort and hotels
- Beachcomber hotels
- Best western
- Britannia hotels
- Canad inns
- Candlewood suites
- Clarion hotels
- Comfort inn
- Comfort suites
- Conrad hotels
- Crowne plaza
- Days inn
- Doubletree
- Drury hotels
- Dusit hotels

- Econo lodge
- Embassy suites
- Etap hotel
- Express by holiday inn
- Fairmont hotels and resorts
- Folio hotels
- Four points by sheraton
- Four seasons hotel
- Golden tulip
- Hampton inn
- Hawthorn suites
- Heartland inn
- Hilton hotels
- Hilton garden inn
- Holiday inn
- Homewood suites by hilton
- Hotel indigo
- Hyatt
- Howard johnson's
- Iberostar
- Ibis
- InterContinental
- Kempinski hotels
- Le meridien
- Loews hotels
- Mainstay suites
- Mandarin oriental
- Marriott international
- Maybourne hotel group
- Microtel inns & suites
- Motel 6
- Mövenpick hotels & resorts
- Morgans hotel group
- Novotel
- Oberoi hotels

- Ohana hotels
- Omni hotels
- Orient-Express hotels
- Outrigger hotels and resorts
- Paradores in puerto rico
- Phoenix inn suites
- Poseidon resorts
- Premier travel inn
- The peninsula hotels
- Quality inn
- Radisson hotels
- Ramada
- Ramada jarvis
- Ritz-carlton
- RIU hotels
- Rocco forte hotels
- Rodeway inn
- St. Regis hotels
- Scandic hotels
- Shangri-La hotels and resorts
- Sheraton hotels and resorts
- Sleep inn
- Sofitel
- Sol Meliá hoteles
- Staybridge suites
- Stamford hotel
- Starwood hotels and resorts worldwide
- Super 8
- Swallow hotels
- Thon hotels
- Travellers inn
- Travelodge
- U.S. franchise systems, inc.
- Victoria inn
- Village hotels

- W. hotel
- Westin hotels.

LODGING AND ITS TYPOLOGY: AN OVERVIEW

Lodging or *holiday accommodation* is a type of accommodation. People who travel and stay away from home for more than a day need *lodging* mainly for sleeping. Other purposes are safety, shelter from cold and rain, having a place to store luggage and being able to take a shower.

They do that in a hotel, hostel or hostal, a private home (commercially, *i.e.* a bed and breakfast or guest house place, vacation rental, or non-commercially, with members of hospitality services or in the home of friends), in a tent, caravan/camper (often on a campsite). In addition there are make-shift solutions.

Sleeping is typically done lying in a bed, or more generally on a soft surface, such as also an air mattress, a couch, etc. Some trains have sleeping cars.

Sometimes people sleep sitting, because lying is not possible, *e.g.* in a train (if not in a sleeping car), a bus, a seat in a waiting room, a bench on the street or in a park, etc. Inclinable seats allow something between sitting and lying. Whether lying on a row of seats is possible and comfortable depends *e.g.*, on the presence of arm rests, and whether they can be moved up. In some public places lying would be possible but is not permitted.

Lodging may also refer to when cereal crops fall over, often due to wind or rain pressure, making grain harvest difficult.

History of Lodging

2000 Occupancy—63 per cent $97 billion in sales New construction will slow from 145,000 in 1999 to 135,000 in 2000	Hilton unveils plans for the first luxury hotel in space.
1990 Occupancy—64 per	1990 : Loews Hotels' Good Neighbour Policy becomes the industry's first and most comprehensive community

(*Contd.*)

cent $60.7 billion in sales Total hotel rooms—3,065,685 45,020 properties Average room rate—$58.70	outreach programme. 1991 : Westin is the first hotel chain to provide in-room voice mail. Industry sees record losses, 61.8 per cent. 1992 : Industry breaks even financially after six consecutive years of losses. 1993 : Radisson Hotels Worldwide is the first to introduce business—classrooms. 1994 : First online hotel catalog debuts: TravelWeb.com. Promus and Hyatt Hotels are the first chains to establish a site on the Internet. 1995 : Choice Hotels International and Promus become the first companies to offer guests "real-time" access to its central reservations system. Choice and Holiday Inn are the first to introduce online booking capability. 1996 : Best Western celebrates its 50th anniversary, making it the oldest continually operating brand. 1999 : Choice Hotels International is the first chain to test making in-room PCs a standard amenity for guests. Starwood Hotels and Resorts takes the boutique segment mainstream with the opening of its W brand.
1980 Occupancy—70 per cent $25.9 billion in sales Total hotel rooms—2,068,377 Average room rate—$45.44	1983 : Westin is the first major hotel company to offer reservations and checkout using major credit cards. VingCard invents the optical electronic key card. 1984 : Holiday Inn is the first to offer a centralized travel agent commission plan. Choice Hotels introduces the concept of market segmentation. Choice Hotels offers no-smoking rooms. Hampton Inns is the first to offer a set of amenities. Holiday Inn debuts Embassy Suites Hotels, the first nationwide all-suite hotel chain, in Overland Park, Kan. 1986 : Teledex Corporation introduces the first telephone designed specifically for hotel guestrooms. Days Inn provides an interactive reservations capability connecting all hotels. 1988 : Extended stay segment introduced with Marriott's Residence Inns and Holiday Corporation's Homewood Suites. 1989 : Hyatt introduces a chainwide kids programme for ages 3-12 and a business centre at the Hyatt Regency Chicago. Hampton Inns is the first hotel chain to introduce the 100 per cent satisfaction guarantee.
1970 Occupancy—65 per cent $8 billion in sales Total hotel rooms—1,627,473	1970 : Hilton becomes the first billion-dollar lodging and food service company and the first to enter the Las Vegas market. Cecil B. Day opens the first Days Inn on Tybee Island, Ga. 1973 : The Sheraton-Anaheim is the first to offer free in-room movies.

(*Contd.*)

Average room rate—$19.83	1974 : The energy crisis hits the industry—hotels dim exterior signs, cut heat to unoccupied rooms, and ask guests to conserve electricity. 1975 : Lodging magazine is authorized as the official publication of AH&MA. Four Seasons is the first hotel company to offer in-room amenities such as name-brand shampoo. Hyatt introduces an industry first when it opens its Regency Club, a concierge club level that provides the ultimate in VIP services. Cecil B. Day hands out wooden nickels to guests over 50, establishing the first seniors programme. 1976 : Two Florida hotels are the first to offer HBO in guestrooms. 1977 : Showtime and The Movie Channel debut in hotels. 1979 : Hyatt names its first woman general manager, Cheryl Phelps, to the former Queen Mary Hyatt in Long Beach, Calif.
1960 Occupancy—67 per cent $3 billion in sales Total hotel rooms—2,400,450 Average room rate—$10.81 Typical hotel—39 rooms, independent, and locally owned	Early 1960s : Siegas introduces the first true minibar (a smal refrigerator displaying products). 1962 : Curt Carlson buys shares of The Radisson Hotel in Minneapolis, Minn. Motel 6, the forerunner of budget brands, opens in Santa Barbara, Calif. 1963 : AHA changes its name to the American Hotel & Lodging Association Desegregation in hotels has started. 1964 : Travelodge debuts wheelchair-accessible rooms. 1966 : Best Western becomes the first hotel company to be wholly governed by a board of directors made up entirely of its own member hoteliers. Inter-Continental introduces retractable drying lines in guest showers, business lounges, ice and vending machines in guest corridors, and street entrances for hotel restaurants. 1967 : The Atlanta Hyatt Regency opens, featuring a 21-story atrium and changing the course of upscale hotel design. Hyatt Hotels Corporation splits into a real-estate holding company. 1969 : Westin is the first hotel chain to implement 24-hour room service.
1950 Occupancy—80 per cent Typical motel—17 rooms Average room rate—$5.91	1951 : The American Hotel Institute, later to be renamed the Educational Institute, is launched. Hilton is the first chain to install television sets in all guestrooms. 1952 : Kemmons Wilson opens his first Holiday Inn in Memphis, Tenn., named after a Bing Crosby movie. 1953 : AHA buys the Universal Credit Card. The American Hotel Foundation, a subsidiary of AHA, is founded. 1954 : Howard Dearing Johnson initiates the first lodging franchise, a motor lodge in Savannah, Ga. Conrad

(*Contd.*)

	Hilton's purchase of the Statler Hotel Company for $111 million is largest real-estate transaction in history. An inn in Flagstaff, Ariz., is the first in a series of "motor hotels" forming Ramada, a Spanish word meaning "a shaded resting place." Mid-1950s : Atlas Hotels develops the first in-room coffee concept. 1957 : J.W. Marriott opens his first hotel, the Twin Bridges Marriott Motor Hotel in Arlington, Va., and Jay Pritzker buys his first hotel, The Hyatt House, located outside the Los Angeles Airport. Hilton offers direct-dial telephone service. 1958 : AHA sells license for the Universal Travel Card to American Express. Sheraton introduces Reservation, the industry's first automated electronic reservations system, and the first toll-free reservation number. Omni Hotels, originally Dunfey Hotels, is founded.
1940 Occupancy—64 per cent Average room rate—$3.21	1940 : Air conditioning and "air cooling" become prevalent. 1945 : Sheraton is the first hotel corporation to be listed on the New York Stock Exchange. Travelodge becomes the first economy lodging corporation. 1946 : Westin debuts first guest credit card. Best Western is founded by M.K. Guertin and 54 friends. Occupancy reaches the highest-ever rate, 93 per cent. The first casino hotel, the Flamingo, debuts in Las Vegas. Larry and Bob Tisch purchase Laurel-in-the-Pines, Lakewood, N.J., which evolved into Loews Hotels. 1947 : Westin establishes Hoteltype, the first hotel reservation system. New York City's Roosevelt Hotel installs television sets in all guestrooms. 1949 : Hilton becomes the first international hotel chain with the opening of the Caribe Hilton in San Juan, Puerto Rico.
1930 Occupancy—65 per cent AHA's Hotel Red Book lists 20,000 hotels Typical hotel—46 rooms Average room rate—$5.60	1930 : Four out of five hotels in the United States go into receivership. The standard travel agent commission is 10 per cent. 1931 : AHA's Chain Hotel Systems debuts, later known as the Directory of Hotel & Motel Companies. 1933 : Due to the Great Depression, hotels post the lowest average occupancy rate on record, 51 per cent Construction grinds to a halt. 1934 : The Hotel Statler in Detroit is the first to have a central system to "air condition" every public room. 1937 : Membership in the Waiters and Bartenders National Union, which encompasses hotel employees, exceeds 200,000. 1939 : Quality Courts, later Choice Hotels International, is formed by seven motel operators as a non-profit

(*Contd.*)

	referral system.
1920 Occupancy—85 per cent Hotel construction reaches an all-time peak as thousands of rooms are added along the new state and federal highways	1920 : Prohibition begins. 1922 : The Treadway Company has some of the first management contracts on small college inns. The first collegiate programme in hotel and restaurant management is initiated at Cornell University by the American Hotel Association. 1925 : The first roadside "motel" opens in San Luis Obispo, Calif., for $2.50 a night. 1927 : The Hotel Statler in Boston becomes the first hotel with radio reception; rooms are equipped with individual headsets to receive broadcasts from a central control room. The American Hotel Association merges with the Hotel Red Book, first printed in 1886. The Huntington Hotel in Calif. installs the first Olympic-size hotel swimming pool. 1928 : There are more than 580,000 industry employees. 1929 : Western Hotels, now Westin, starts with 17 hotels in the Pacific Northwest and establishes the first U.S. hotel management company. The Oakland Airport Hotel becomes the first of its kind in the country.
1910 10,000 U.S. hotels One million rooms 300,000 employees Average size—60-75 rooms	1910 : The American Hotel Protective Association is founded in Chicago. The lodging industry consists almost entirely of hotels situated in urban centres and resorts near the principal vacation destinations. Electricity is beginning to be installed in new hotels for cooking purposes, as well as for lighting. However, most hotels place candlesticks, new candles, and matches in every room- electric light bulb or not. 1916 : The Federal Road Aid Act spawns a new segment of the lodging industry. 1917 : The American Hotel Protective Association changes its name to the American Hotel Association (AHA) of the United States and Canada. 1919 : Conrad Hilton purchases his first hotel, The Mobley, in Cisco, Texas.
1900 Fewer than 10,000 hotels 750,000 to 850,000 rooms	1900 : A typical first-class hotel offers steam heat, gas burners, electric call bells, baths and closets on all floors, billiard and sample rooms, barbershops, and liveries. The Lenox Hotel, known today as The Lenox Hotel and Suites/Village Lodge, offered "fireproof lodging, unexcelled cuisine, a shower bath, roof garden, and American/European lodging plans starting at $2." 1904 : New York City's St. Regis Hotel provides individually controlled heating and cooling units in each guestroom.

(*Contd.*)

	Superior Hotel in Montana. The Hotel Statier chain begins in Buffalo. All guestrooms have private baths, full-length mirrors, telephones, and built-in radios, serving as the model for hotel construction for the next 40 years.

List of Lodging Types

This is a selected **list of types of lodging**. Items on this list should be types of lodging, however loosely defined.

- Airport
- Airplane
- Apartment hotel
- Apartment
- Barn conversion
- Barracks
- Bed and breakfast, or B&B
- Bedsit
- Boarding house
- Bothy
- Bungalow
- Bus
- Bus station
- Bus stop
- Camper, Caravan, Recreational vehicle or Trailer
- Capsule hotel
- Car
- Caravan parks
- Casino hotel
- Cave
- Cell (prison)
- Chambre d'hôtes
- Choultry
- Condominium, or Timeshare
- Cottage
- County jail

- Dormitory
- Extended stay hotel
- Flophouse
- Guest House or Guesthouse
- Hospital
- Hospitality services
- Hostel
- Hotel
- House
- Igloo
- Inn
- Lavvu, Sami tent
- Log cabin
- Love hotel, fashion hotel, boutique hotel
- Mini dorm
- Minshuku
- Monastery
- Motel
- Longhouse
- No tell-Motel
- Nursing home
- Palace
- Pension
- Prison
- Public house
- Public housing
- Public transport
- Psychiatric hospital
- Ramada (shelter)
- Resort
- Retirement home
- Ryokan, a traditional Japanese inn
- Sanatorium
- Single Room Occupancy
- Sleeping car on a Train
- Tent

- Bell tent
    - Bender tent
    - Tipi
    - Wigwam
    - Yurt
- Train station
- Turbaza
- Tree house
- Underground house
- Vacation rental
- Villa

BED AND BREAKFAST

Bed and breakfast, also known as B&B, is a term, originating in the United Kingdom, but now also used in the USA and Canada, for an establishment that offers bed accommodation, and breakfast in return for payment, but usually does not offer other meals. Typically, bed and breakfasts are private homes with only one or two bedrooms available for commercial use.

A boarding house is different from and has a longer history than a bed and breakfast facility. The boarding house is for longer term stays, whereas bed and breakfast is for people travelling through the area on short stays.

Overview

Generally, guests are accommodated in private bedrooms with private bathrooms, or in a suite of rooms including an en suite bathroom. Some homes have private bedrooms with a bathroom which is shared with another guest or sometimes more than one other guest. Breakfast is served in the morning—in the bedroom, a dining room, or the host's kitchen.

B&Bs and guest houses may be operated either as a secondary source of income or a primary occupation. Staff can consist of the home's owners and family members, or you may find some bed and breakfasts where the home's owners have hired cleaning, cooking and other staff. A property which hires professional management is no longer a bed and breakfast, but enters the category of Inn, Guest House or Small Hotel. B&B's are a form of a tertiary business.

National Differences

Australia

Despite the cultural similarities, there are far fewer B&B's in the whole continent of Australia than there are in just the South Island of New Zealand despite the resident population being more than twenty times greater.

Since 1879, the average per capita disposable income of Australians has been greater than that of New Zealanders and this has mitigated the powerful incentive to let out rooms in their homes to travellers. Another factor may be that Australia has, apart from City States such as Singapore, the greatest concentration of city dwellers anywhere on the globe and these cities are amply supplied with budget hotels and motels.

Belgium

In Belgium bed and breakfasts generally offer better value than hotels, and provide the opportunity to sample the local food and meet new people. Bed and breakfast accommodations often have a very relaxing, homey feel to them.

Britain and Ireland

B&Bs, and frequently, guest houses, are a budget option where owners often take pride in the high service levels, local knowledge and personal touch that they are able to offer.

There tend to be concentrations of B&Bs in the seaside towns where, historically, the working classes holidayed such as Newcastle in Ireland and Blackpool in England, in isolated rural areas such as the Highlands of Scotland and Connemara where there is not a year-round concentration of travellers sufficient to sustain an hotel, and are present in most towns and cities in numbers dependent upon factors such as the level of tourism,

York in England and Edinburgh in Scotland, for example, both have several hundred establishments known as either B&B's or guest houses.

Breakfast is usually cooked on demand for the guest and usually features bacon, eggs, sausages, tomatoes, mushrooms and baked beans, but some offer a continental breakfast.

In recent years some bed and breakfast businesses in the UK have struggled against budget hotel chains such as Premier Travel Inn and Travelodge. Traditionally, business travellers used B&Bs but many of these clients now tend to stay in budget hotel chains. However, in holiday areas the B&B and guest house still prevails. Unlike the 'chain' accommodation providers these provide a more comprehensive service and breakfast is included in the price.

Cuba

In Cuba, which opened up to tourism in the 1990s after the financial support of the Soviet Union ended, a form of B&B called *casa particular* ("private home") became the main form of accommodation outside the tourist resorts.

Israel

The Israeli B&B is known as a *zimmer* (German for *room*). All over the country, but especially in the north of the country and the Galilee, *zimmers* have become a popular alternative to hotels for romantic weekends cr family vacations.

New Zealand

As in the USA, Bed and Breakfasts in New Zealand tend to be more expensive than Motels and often feature historic homes and lovingly furnished bedrooms at a commensurate price. The historic city of Nelson has an unusually high concentration of both of these accommodations and alternatives because it was historically the place where kiwis holidayed.

North America

Many B&Bs in North America try to create a historical ambiance, with old properties turned into guest houses decorated with antique furniture. For example, the Holladay House in Orange, Virginia is an 1830s Federal-style brick building that has been converted into a bed and breakfast. Recently, B&B and Inn owners have been launching upscale amenities to improve business and move "up-market." It is not uncommon now to find free wireless Internet access, free parking, spa services, or nightly wine and cheese hours. Due to the need to stay competitive with the rest of the lodging industry, larger bed and breakfast inns have expanded to offer wedding services, business conference facilities, and meeting spaces as well as many other services a large hotel might offer.

Regulations

Regulations and laws vary considerably in each national jurisdiction both in content and extent and in enforcement.

The most common regulations B&Bs must follow pertain to safety. They are usually required by local and national ordinances to have fire resistance, a sufficient fire escape plan in place, and smoke detectors in each guestroom. Kitchens and equipment used to serve meals are also often required to be monitored for hygienic operation, but there are significant national and local differences. Most B&Bs are generally compliant with their jurisdiction's laws.

In Hawaii, it is illegal to open an new bed and breakfast on Oahu as of 1989. The reason for the moratorium is to force home owners with extra room to rent out their extra space to low income residents who otherwise cannot afford housing on crowded Oahu.

National Associations

While various local governments have regulations and inspect for health issues and fire safety code, membership in a state/provincial/national bed and breakfast association can indicate a higher standard of hospitality. Associations sometimes review their members' properties and tend to have additional standards of care.

These associations also facilitate marketing of the individual B&Bs and provide a stamp of approval that the business in question is reputable. This "stamp of approval", however, may be just an indication that membership dues have been paid.

USA

Two for-profit professional *innkeeper* associations that operate in the United States are the Professional Association of Innkeepers International and Select Registry. Most states also have state associations. These associations are usualy non-profit organizations.

The Professional Association of Innkeepers International (PAII) is a national for-profit organization with members in the U.S., Canada, and other countries. PAII currently holds annual trade conferences for education of innkeepers and prospective innkeepers. Attendance to these conferences is open and well advertised to all. PAII also provides an industry study to all of its members at low cost that details operations and finance of the industry.

Select Registry is a *national* organization that inspects its member properties on a regular basis, beyond routine inspections that may be carried out by the local government.

The Caucus of American Innkeepers (or CAIK) is a social and professional networking organization for owners of B&Bs, country inns, and similar properties.

The Bettina Network, is a national network of private homes which accept bed and breakfast guests. All homes are thoroughly checked out by someone from the Network spending the night in the home. The network handles all aspects of the room (pricing, advertising, reservations, payment collection etc). Questionnaires are sent to each guest to insure the satisfaction of all who use the service.

In the US, states also have innkeeping associations that are usually non-profit and exist to promote the industry and state tourism. However, many state associations, such as the Bed and Breakfast Association of Virginia (BBAV) have rigorous inspection criteria that often exceed government requirements for safety and cleanliness.

Chapter 2

Hotel and Hospitality Services Management: Issues and Areas

HOSPITALITY SERVICE

The concept of Hospitality Services, also known as "accommodation sharing", "hospitality exchange", and "home stay networks", refers to centrally organized social networks of individuals who trade accommodation without monetary exchange. While this conceptualization could also include house swapping or even time share plans, it has come to be associated mostly with travellers and tourists staying with one another free of charge. Since the 1990s, these services have increasingly moved away from using printed catalogues and phone trees to connect users towards Internet websites to store info in databases. They have grown exponentially since 2000 and today it is estimated that well over 100,000 people are registered users of these networks. These vary in operational structure, place different emphasis on graphical vs. textual formatting, and cater disproportionately to specific geographic regions.

History

In 1949, Bob Luitweiler founded the first hospitality service called Servas Open Doors as a cross national, non-profit, volunteer run organization advocating interracial and international peace. The next earliest began in 1965 when John Wilcock set up the Traveller's Directory, originally as a listing of his mutual friends willing to host each other when travelling. This later became the Hospitality Exchange in 1988 when Joy

Lily rescued the organization from imminent demise. Hospitality Club is the direct successor Hospex, the first Internet-based service, operating out of Poland since 1992. It is currently the largest hospitality exchange network, growing rapidly. CouchSurfing is a newer but also rapidly growing hospitality exchange organization founded in 2004. Just as all the individual services have their own individual creation stories and organizational histories (often including demise and resurrection), many also have specific niche markets that they cater to including students, activists, religious pilgrims, and even occupational groups like police officers. However, the trend in recent years points to a greater consolidation of users in networks without an overt group, value, or lifestyle affiliation.

How they Work?

In essence, these systems employ fundamental reciprocity—users gain access to other users' information only by posting their own. Requisite fields normally include name and contact information, though newer services encourage users to include more detailed personal material, including likes and dislikes, hopes and dreams, and even photographs. Of course, more information included tends to improve the chances that someone will find them trustworthy enough to host or stay with while travelling. It is very much akin to today's online dating services.

Benefits

Monetary Savings

Staying in private homes means that travellers can save lots of money on accommodation that they would usually be spending on hotels or hostels. Used over a long period of time (2 to 4 weeks), this strategy can cut overall travel budgets in half, or even more combined with hitchhiking. These savings can then be passed on towards more generously patronizing local establishments or simply staying abroad for longer periods of time, which is said to make the tourist experience significantly more authentic.

Local Economic Sustainability

Many tourist vacations today are sold in package form, often including flights, hotels, rental cars, sightseeing tours, and coupons for chain restaurants and bars. While this makes purchasing more convenient, it also puts more money in the hands of large multinational corporations exploiting the synergy strategy of marketing their products in the context of their subsidiary companies operating in other markets. Many years ago, this might have been termed *collusion*; today, however, it is the norm. This comes at the expense of locally owned independent businesses. Accommodation sharing helps to break apart this monopoly and hopefully redirects some of the tourist revenue back to the local or national economy.

Ecological Sustainability

While this is especially important in more rural travel venues where hotels are often built in very picturesque, though fragile environments, every night stayed at a local's home means that much less demand for such hotel rooms. Also, if accommodation sharing does in fact increase the length of average stays, it may reduce the amount of trips to and from different locations and back home again, thus reducing the overall fuel expenditures in the process.

Local Contact

Ostensibly, one of the primary reasons we travel is to experience what life is like for people living in other countries. Making interpersonal connections and fostering understanding of different cultures may in the long run also be important to international relations. However, even in our increasingly globalized world supposedly rife with diversity, in many popular travel destinations we find tourists milling around "tourist enclaves" where the companies they patronize back home have set up shop to cater to their desires while they are abroad. Sociologist George Ritzer has referred to this phenomenon as the "McDonaldisation of society" and the more recently, the "globalization of nothing". The location of hotels near these centres only fosters more convenient envelopment of the tourist dollar. During hospitality exchanges, hosts want to show off their local knowledge and exciting "off the map" venues. Not only will travellers get a distinctly different experience, but they will also get a feel for the everyday lives of local residents.

Reciprocity

These systems foster richer and more convenient travel experiences not so much on the premise of altruism, but on the basis of social exchange theory. Implicit in the agreement to host travellers is the ability to ask to be hosted by them in the future. If one enjoys having interesting guests in their home, this works out well for both parties. It works comparatively better if you are visited by travellers from a locale you find particularly attractive. Thus, hosting someone from New York City in Gainesville, FL seems to be an unbelievable opportunity. Moreover, if you are a Westerner visiting someone in a developing nation, your stay might be the only way that this individual or family could afford a trip to a rich nation. This may mean more than just a relaxing vacation for such disadvantaged parties.

Authenticity and Adventure

Tourism has always searched for these two qualities, but much like Midas and his golden touch, the reach of tourism has to a large extent destroyed the opportunity to encounter them in most places. Unluckily, the experience has been thoroughly commodified by everyone who wanted to secure their opportunity to make a buck in the process. Accommodation sharing offers a way out of this bind and a viable alternative to having one's desires manipulated by corporate conglomerates who never had the best interests of the place or the people foremost in their minds.

Drawbacks

Lack of Guarantee

There is no contractual agreement between users in these systems. Reservations are made, but if they are for some reason broken, there is no higher authority to which one could plead for a refund or other compensation. The only repercussion will be the poor rating you give that user and your only consolation will be that your warning will deter others from visiting or hosting them. For those who feel insecure unless their travel arrangements are written in stone before departure, this system will not be comforting.

Potential Interpersonal Conflict or Awkwardness

There is a chance that guest and host will not get along. Perhaps there will be scheduling or ideological conflicts. Maybe you will find that hosts or visitors have misrepresented themselves. Perhaps the experience will not live up to your expectations. Intense interpersonal communications in advance and a flexibility once you have arrived is your best bet. These experiences require additional planning and courtesy towards the demands of your host. Thus, your living conditions, length of stay, and overall experience will be circumscribed by the living conditions you enter into.

Digital Divide and Demographic Segregation

The average user is a young white person who speaks English and lives in a developed nation. While there are many users who do not fit this description, the more different they are, the less likely they will be involved. This is especially true for persons living in the developing world who likely do not have easy access to the fundamental prerequisite for using these services: computers and the Internet. Thus, the sample population found in searches of these databases are really much less diverse than a geographical representation of worldwide users might suggest.

Security

Everyone realizes there is a distinct possibility that someone will abuse the system and that innocent users (especially women) will get hurt. All services include disclaimers that require users to waive their rights to hold anyone but themselves responsible for any harm that may come to them in using the system. They advise that the best defense mechanism is to only involve oneself with users that have extensive personal information and interpersonal networks within the system that have been verified by others. It does seem entirely plausible that someone clever and patient enough might be able to invent an entire group of complex user identities and build histories convincing enough to fool even more cautious patrons. Still, the difference between these systems and the other social networking platforms popular now-a-days on the web (such as MySpace, Tribe, Orkut, LiveJournal and Ebay) is that any agreement reached through the accommodation sharing medium is contingent on actually meeting other people face-to-face. Other web scams are easier because interpersonal interactions rely so much on putative identities that are never actually verified in the real world. However, this does not diminish the greater risk to physical well-being that this kind of travelling by definition must entertain. The best advice is to meet unknown persons in public spaces first, and try to meet some of their acquaintances in person before agreeing to a hospitality exchange.

Single Room Occupancy

The expression "single room occupancy" or, more commonly "SRO", refers to a building that houses people in single rooms. This means that tenants must share bathrooms and kitchens. The term originated in New York City, probably in the 1930s (the Oxford English Dictionary provides an earliest citation of 1941), but the institutions date back at least fifty years before the nickname was applied to them. SROs exist in many large American cities. The terms single room occupancy and SRO are not used in British English. Related British terms include house in multiple occupation, hostel and bedsit.

In many cases, the buildings themselves were formerly hotels in or near a city's central business district. Others are former single family homes. Many of these buildings were built in the late 19th and early 20th centuries, and reflect a high order of architectural style and craftsmanship. In the United States, the decades from the 1920s onward saw the movement of the upper classes, who lived in these homes and occupied the hotels, to the suburbs. A process often referred to as "filtering" resulted in the occupancy of these buildings and districts by the lower socio-economic classes. Though the facilities do not receive the same standard of maintenance once they become SROs, often enough of the old opulance remains to create an ironic contrast with the tenants who live there.

Typically, the residents in SROs are men who are impoverished, debilitated, mentally ill, addicted to drugs, and/or dying. However, SROs are also a viable housing option for some students, divorcees, and professionals who are willing to suffer the disadvantages of living in an SRO in exchange for lower rent and the weekly or monthly leasing periods such facilities may allow. By contrast, apartment leases are typically for one year.

The rents of many tenants are paid by state and federal programmes, eliminating much of the unease that might otherwise have prevented landlords from accepting these tenants. As a result, the buildings operate essentially as private homeless shelters. See, for example, Section 441 of the McKinney-Vento Homeless Assistance Act.

Depending on the sensibilities of the landlords and the quality of the properties, SROs can range from Dickensian squalor to something like a very low end tourist hotel. Some have been run in dormitory fashion. Others have been "cage" hotels, in which a large room is split into many smaller ones with corrogated steel or sheetrock dividers, which do not reach the height of the original ceiling. To prevent tenants from climbing over the walls into each others' spaces, the tops of the rooms are covered in chicken wire, making the rooms look something like cages.

As the value of urban land has increased, it has become economical to renovate these properties and make them available once again to higher bidders. This has displaced the people who once lived in them, and is one of the reasons for the visible increase in the population of homeless in the streets of American cities since the early 1980s.

Recognizing that there is significant incentive for landlords to forcibly evict SRO tenants in gentrifying neighbourhoods, the city of New York applies strict rules to the conversion of SROs to other use. In particular, if tenants testify that they have been harassed in any way, conversion can be delayed by three years. Landlords who intend to convert SROs usually try to convince their tenants to sign releases, which may require finding them new places to live and/or paying them.

San Francisco similarly passed an SRO Hotel Conversion Ordinance in 1980, which restricts the conversion of SRO hotels to tourist use. SROs are prominent in the Tenderloin, Mission District and Chinatown communities. In 2001, San Francisco Supervisor Chris Daly sponsored legislation making it illegal for SRO landlords to charge "visitor fees"—a practice long run in order for hotel managers to get a "cut" on drug-dealing or prostitution activities in the building.

Vacation Rental

Vacation rental is a term in the travel industry meaning renting out a furnished apartment or house on a temporary basis to tourists as an alternative to a hotel. Vacation rentals are becoming increasingly popular in Europe (especially in the UK) as well as in Canada. In some cities, like Barcelona, local authorities determined that vacation rentals were becoming a threat to the hotel industry, and passed some legislation placing regulations and limits on the industry.

Differences between Vacation Rentals and Timeshares

Consumers unfamiliar with the concept of a vacation rental may confuse it with the seemingly similar, but distinctly different, timeshare.

A *timeshare* is a piece of real estate—often a condominium—that is jointly shared by multiple owners. While different types of timeshare ownerships exist, in general, each owner bears a portion of the responsibility, along with the right to a segment of time in which he or she is granted sole use of the property. Timeshare resorts allow financially qualified guests to rent and tour their unowned properties and then make those properties available to the guest for purchase.

Similarly, a **vacation rental** is a fully furnished property, such as a condominium, townhome or single-family-style home. However, a true vacation rental is not for sale to the guest; rather, the owner of the vacation rental merely allows the guest to rent the property for a predetermined length of time.

Pros and Cons of Vacation Rentals

In the United States, hotels often enjoy the advantages of brand recognition, familiar reservation processes and on-site staff for problem resolution. For a guest, booking a vacation rental often meant stepping out of that comfort zone. Perceived cons of vacation rentals include: having to communicate directly with the property owner, being unfamiliar with the property, lack of on-site staff and concerns about quality or cleanliness.

However, for some guests, the benefits outweigh the potential negatives, with many vacation rentals offering more space (multiple bedrooms and bathrooms, separate living areas), more amenities (fully equipped kitchens, fireplaces, private hot tubs), convenient locations (on the beach, ski-in/ski-out) and greater privacy than a hotel. As of 2006, vacation rental management has become a $10 billion industry.

Vacation Rental Management Companies

Many property owners contract a vacation rental management company to manage the business of their vacation rentals. These management companies market the vacation rental property, providing information and photos to guests and handling reservations and billing in the homeowner's stead. These companies also handle details such as guest check-in, housekeeping and property maintenance.

The largest vacation rental property management company in the United States represents nearly 17,000 vacation rental properties. Guests who book through vacation rental management companies may experience benefits including quality control, housekeeping services, professional reservations agents and on-site or on-call staff.

Listing Services and Aggregators

Aside from those represented by a few large property management companies, vacation rentals may be offered through aggregation portals. Aggregators typically display property information and photos provided by the homeowner, however the listing services bear no legal responsibility for the accuracy of the information. Also, because the listing services do not verify the information, they strongly encourage guests to request references from past renters and to procure a lease agreement prior to sending money to a homeowner.

A vacation rental may not be booked directly with a listing service. Because each property owner has his or her own deposit and payment requirements, cancellation policies, key-pick-up procedures, etc., a guest must contact the property owner or owner's agent directly in order to book.

RevPAR

RevPAR, or revenue per available room, is an important metric relevant to the hotel industry. Often it is utilized as a primary statistic indicating the overall financial performance of a property.

Note that RevPAR numbers represent a measure of performance in terms relative to a property's past results, and especially in comparison to competitors within a custom defined market, trading area, or DMA. Also, comparisons are usually best considered between hotels of the same type, or with target customers (*e.g.* Full Service, Luxury, Extended Stay, Economy).

A few syndicated data companies compile RevPAR information across markets via voluntary survey, and provide compiled blinded information back to the industry.

Other Caveats

- Successful RevPAR numbers differ from market to market based on demand, cost of living, and other factors.
- Best compared across like time periods. For example, it is proper to compare RevPAR on a Friday only *vs.* other Fridays.
- Best compared across similar seasonal time periods. For example, comparing results from the Christmas week with the same a year previous is more credible than with a non-holiday week.

Calculation

- *RevPAR* is revenue per available room,
- *A* is the ADR, the average price per room sold,
- 0 per cent is the rate of occupancy, or per cent of rooms sold.

GUEST REVENUE IN RESORT HOTELS

Predictions of a 5 per cent growth in leisure vacations along with recommendations to focus on total guest revenues highlighted the 6th Annual Resort Management Conference presented by the Hospitality Sales and Marketing Association International (HSMAI) the University of Denver School of Hotel, Restaurant and Tourism Management (HRTM) and the International Resort Managers Association (IRMA) at Pinehurst Resort, North Carolina, last week. The latest research and travel trends, success stories and best practices, marketing innovations and new operational ideas headlined the agenda for a record number of 202 attendees representing nearly 50 independent resorts and 17 management companies and ownership groups. "This year's Resort Conference not only had a record attendance, but had the highest evaluation scores of any of the five previous conferences held to date," said Robert A. Gilbert, CHME, CHA, President and CEO of HSMAI. "The 2006 Resort Management Conference delivered outstanding programming to educate and inform, as well as unprecedented attendance for networking," said James H. Johnson, Executive Director, International Resort Managers Association. "In just a few years, the Conference has become an industry 'must-do,'" he added.

> "This conference, produced as a cooperative partnership between HSMAI, IRMA and our Hotel, Restaurant and Tourism Management School, brought together three entities that resulted in an outstanding event for all delegates," said Peter Rainsford, Director, School of Hotel, Restaurant and Tourism Management, Daniels College of Business, University of Denver.

General Session: Travel Trends

Peter Yesawich, President and CEO of Yesawich, Pepperdine, Brown and Russell, predicted a 5 per cent growth in leisure vacation travel as he presented research about both business and leisure travel trends including:

- Predicting 5 per cent growth of vacationing in America in the next 12 months (37% say they will travel the same amount, 29 % said less, 34% said more).
- Of the 29 per cent who said they will travel less, 25 per cent cited household economic conditions, and 24 per cent said they are not able to get away from their job.
- Time poverty is continuing to reinvent the way Americans vacation.
- Family travel is the only category of leisure travel that is increasing with more parents travelling with children including some as extensions of business trips.
- In the latest Travel Monitor, 36 per cent took vacation with kids, and 61 per cent of parents said they were willing to take their kids out of school for a vacation.

"Volunteer Vacations is a new category and a growing number of people have taken a vacation to help the less fortunate or support a cause," said Yesawich.

"Group meetings are shorter – therefore more accessible locations are doing better," noted John Beckert, President and CEO, Club Corp, Inc.

As family vacations continue to grow, "it is very important for us to offer both family time and adult time for families on vacation," said Dr. Richard Kelley, Chairman & CEO, Outrigger Hotels and Resorts.

Meanwhile, a cautionary note was issued that "our biggest challenge is that our sale is a personal sale, but there is a lot of turnover in those sales people," said Charles S. Peck, President and CEO, Destination Hotels and Resorts. "Talent is the biggest issue and the pool of talented/qualified people is not growing," Peck said. "As an industry we need to address that," he urged.

Jan Freitag, Director of client services, Smith Travel Research, gave this analysis of the state of the resort industry today:

- ❖ Life is good, but we are not quite back to the heydays of the mid-1990s, mostly due to the amount of inventory that has come online in the last 10 years.
- ❖ We think rate growth is here to stay for at least the rest of the year, and probably next year.
- ❖ Occupancy still has a ways to go to recover.
- ❖ Our occupancy forecast for resorts in 2006 is 64.3 per cent and 8.0 per cent RevPar growth.

Maximizing Ancillary Revenue in a Resort

How to Find Your Hidden Sources?

Capitalizing on potential revenue sources, discovering hidden potential revenue sources outside and within the resort business unit, learning about everything from outlet point of sale incentive programmes to comprehensive retail strategies and the marketing concepts that drive them is what experts shared through case studies and best practices of successful resorts.

"There is a new emphasis today on total guest revenue," urged Terri A. Haack, Vice-President and Managing Director, Wild Dunes Resort and Destination Hotels and Resorts.

Recommendations for increasing ancillary revenue came from a number of panelists including: Pam Streeter, Vice-President of electronic distribution, Interstate Hotels and Resorts:

1. Try to capture ancillary revenue at the time of booking by allowing guests to make reservations for ancillary services (spa, golf, restaurants, etc.) online at the time they book their stay.
2. Make sure information about these services and information about how to book are very visible on your Website.
3. Allow people to prepay when they make their reservations for things such as telecommunications services (Internet connection, phone calls, etc.), pet care, in room gaming/movies.

Stephen H. Baldwin, President, Stephen H. Baldwin Retail Development Co., noted that shopping is the number one leisure activity in the U.S. and suggested:

1. Create concepts that are right for your property.
2. Create spaces that are custom in look and feel.
3. Overdo your packaging.
4. Create a market concept to have people fill their own minibars.
5. Offer gift cards online, at resort, and with local retailers.

Jaime Huffman, Executive Director, Grove Park Inn Resort, suggested that "Your spa should be a full sensory experience, should be relaxing, pampering and not a hassle." To maximize profitability:

1. Choose the right treatment mix.
2. Know your cost of treatment.
3. Use suggestive selling.
4. Educate employees to do this.

Tjibbe Lambers, Marketing and Promotions Manager, Hershey Resorts, said "To maximize revenue we try to free-up parents to do other activities such as spa, golf and dining, and to do this we opened a kids club." He urged hoteliers to "look for opportunities to add value to the experience that is in keeping with your resort."

Resort Best Practices Initiative

A well-attended session on Resort Best Practices, headed up by Cindy Estis Green, Managing Partner, The Estis Group, exposed delegates to an assortment of examples of Best Practices, details of some of the findings of the first study on Internet marketing, and an overview of results to be released on the recent CRM study.

Members of the HSMAI Best Practices Initiative gave the following examples of actions they have taken as a result of the Internet marketing study:

- Barry Brown, Director of Sales and Marketing, Sanibel Harbour Resort and Spa, said "The findings helped us to layout a 24-month improvement plan for our Internet marketing efforts."
- Tjibbe Lambers, Marketing and Promotions Manager, Hershey Resorts, said "We are now partnering with Google to do search engine optimization."
- Frank Fredericks, Vice-President, Sales and Marketing, Wild Dunes Resort, said "We came away with nine takeaways, including adding e-confirmations and interactive proposals."
- John Washko, Director of Sales and Marketing, the Broadmoor, said "We have realized we need to bring our online silos together."

Hotel and Restaurant Management Training

Employment opportunities in the field of hotel and restaurant management are projected to grow at least as fast as average, according to the U.S. Bureau of Labour Statistics. Salaries tend to be above the national average, at a little less than $40,000. Applicants for management positions do need work experience in order to be promoted. But those with career education in hotel and restaurant management likely will find the best employment opportunities, though no training programme can guarantee a specific salary or a job offer.

Hospitality Career Training

In a career education programme for the hotel and restaurant industry, you'll likely study the following:

- Nutrition
- Sanitation
- Food planning and preparation
- Accounting
- Business law and management
- Commonly used software programmes.

Many career training programmes provide students with the opportunity to earn their diplomas through online programmes. Students who get their education online can work while studying, which can allow individuals to advance in their careers at a faster rate.

Our Featured Education Partners

Penn Foster Career School

Established in 1890, Penn Foster Career School is one of the oldest and largest distance learning institutions in the world. Students can study online, in print, or a combination of each—you decide which method best suits your learning style. Career Diploma and vocational training programmes in catering and hotel management include:

- Catering and Gourmet Cooking.
- Hotel/Restaurant Management.

Penn Foster Career School is accredited by the Middle States Commission on Secondary Schools for high school and vocational-technical programmes, and by the Accrediting Commission of the Distance Education and Training Council (DETC). Penn Foster Career School is affiliated with DANTES, which qualifies U.S. military personnel for tuition reimbursement. Many Penn Foster programmes are approved for U.S. Armed Forces veterans training benefits.

Penn Foster Career School offers affordable, all-inclusive pricing-among the lowest of all career schools—and 0 per cent interest financing and customized payment plans.

E-Learn.uk.com

E-Learn.uk offers distance learning through the Internet, giving students an interactive educational experience and the opportunity to study through highly accredited learning providers. With roughly 500 vocational and career training courses available online, E-Learn.uk offers something for everybody. Offered catering operations and events planning courses include:

- Food and Beverage Management,
- Franchising,
- Guest House Management,
- Hotel Management,
- Restaurant Management, and
- Events Planning.

Students enroll, sign on, and conduct all class activities, from any location in the World, with only a standard Web Browser and without complicated plug-in software and can quickly access your course material on line. You'll learn at your own pace, decide on your own method of learning, all with a choice of payment options. You can work online or print out course materials and get started right away on a new educational experience.

Ashworth University:

Ashworth University is a widely respected, nationally accredited distance education school, and offers the following catering programme:

- Professional Gourmet Cooking and Catering Programme.

Students receive comprehensive texts and study materials by mail, and study in the convenience of home, at their own pace. Exams are open-book. Also available is a home study high school diploma programme from James Madison High School. Monthly tuition is interest free. Students may enroll online, year-round.

Ashworth University is an Accredited Member of the Distance Education and Training Council. The Accrediting Commission of the Distance Education and Training Council is listed by the U.S. Department of Education as a nationally recognized accrediting agency, for distance learning schools. Ashworth University is qualified under the Defense Activity for Non-Traditional Education Support, or DANTES programme. Ashworth University offers easy, interest-free monthly tuition.

Cornell University

The Cornell School of Hotel Administration offers the following certificates online:

- Certification in the Essentials of Hospitality Management.
- Certification in Foodservice Management.

Accredited by the Middle States Association of Colleges and Schools.

e-Drama Learning

e-Drama Learning provides web based customer service learning for the hospitality industry. Your staff can learn Customer Service by interacting with e-Drama's emotional and dramatic virtual guests. e-Drama's web hotel puts hospitality training in a realistic, challenging and fun game-like environment.

HTC Distance Education

HTC distance education has over 40 years of distance education experience and has up-to-date curriculums for the hospitality and tourism fields. HTC enrolls students from across the United States, as well as throughout the world.

Professional Development Institute of Tourism

The professional development institute of Tourism located in British Columbia, Canada, offers several distance learning programmes in hospitality and tourism including:

- Hospitality management diploma.
- Hospitality operations certificate.

PDIT Tourism and Hospitality programmes are industry approved and internationally recognized materials currently used by leading hotel companies, as well as by over 1000 universities, colleges, vocational-technical schools and government agencies world wide. The curriculum is geared to meet the certification requirements of The Hotel Association of Canada, the American Hotel and Lodging Association (AHMA) Educational Institute. The programmes are approved by British Columbia and Yukon Hotels' Association (BCYHA), and Hospitality Industry Education Advisory Committee (HIEAC).

Wine Spectator School

Wine spectator school offers many online wine courses for both consumers and those in the hospitality and wine trade business including:

- Understanding wine,
- ABCs of wine tasting,

- Understanding professional wine sales and service, and
- ABCs of wine sales and service.

Printable reference materials include study guides, class worksheets, portfolio worksheets and tasting notes. Online quizzes and exams verify progress. Students scoring 80 per cent or better on the final exam receive a Wine Spectator School certificate that is suitable for framing.

Travel and Tourism Management

Travel and tourism management is an exciting field involving diverse organization, institutions, board, support network, service specialists and media world to effectively deliver results in the hospitality segment. The scope and potential for travel and tourism management is enormous in complete growth of an economy, country or an industry. It thus plays a great role in shaping our career & has attained significant role in Education Management and Planning.

The comforts work in tandem with State Governments, tourism boards, principals, backend specialist, educational institutions, career planners to offer a complete platform for efficient travel and tourism management in the world. Our specialized segment on destination marketing, country management, event management, career management and education management complement travel and tourism segment in its true potential.

Travel and Tourism Management International Air Travel Support

International airlines of the world, major airports of the world, air travel charter, helicopter travel service, air travel taxi, emergency services, travel specialists and associates in the world, service providers.

Travel and Tourism Management Domestic Air Travel Services

Major airlines of india, major airports of india, air travel charter in India, helicopter travel service in India, air travel taxi, emergency travel services in India, travel specialists in India, travel service support in india.

Travel and Tourism Management Railway Travel Solution Services

Luxury train travel in India and the world, luxury train tour packages for India and world, major railway stations of the world, railway reservation network in India.

Travel and Tourism Management Road Travel Organizations

Car rental specialists, coach rental specialists, fleet operators and hire, road travel packages for India and World.

Travel and Tourism Management Travel by Sea Support Services

Luxury cruise travel and tourism in the world, luxury yacht source guide, sailing terms and sports, ports, major cruise destinations of the world, cruise packages, sea world expeditions, sports and tourism, cruising support, emergency services on high seas, cruise specialists and associates in the world, cruise equipment, cruise useful addresses, medical services and guideline, embarkation, sailing and cruise products.

Travel and Tourism Management Utilities, Facts and Information

Traveller facts, world travel magazines, medical and health guidelines, travel and tourism facilitation, travel useful addresses, visa services, travel insurance, country passport and regulations, catering specialists, world currency, country management.

Travel and Tourism Management Accommodation—Hotel Booking

Luxury resort and spa rejuvenation packages, business hotel stay plans and facilities, heritage property vacation package, luxury hotel stay booking and events, international hotel booking, hotel chain booking and packages.

Travel and Tourism Management: Support Management Services

Event management support, wedding management plan, sports management.

Travel and Tourism Management Theme Vacations and Holidays Plan

Theme holiday packages, UNESCO world heritage sites, spiritualism and religious tourism in the world, rejuvenation, therapeutic and total health management tourism, wild life safaris and tourism, golf tourism, world art and culture, world festivals experience, nature and eco tourism.

The Comforts Services and Options

The comforts combine principled stance, interactive style and professional approach to bring out the complete dossier of products, services, development, institutions and information on Travel and Tourism Management.

The comforts has a dedicated "Buyer-Seller" section called "Interactive Forum" to help facilitate various products and services between the advertisers and those who wish to avail them off under Travel and Tourism Management.

However, the usage under Travel and Tourism Management section is governed by certain "Terms and Conditions" which are applicable for both the buyers and the sellers. One may be required to accept them before proceeding further.

In order to reach the targetted audiences, the comforts offer various cost-effective location, product, services and category specific "Advertising Plans" for the advertisers and promoters. Join us for a wonderful experience of co-promotion with us. Lets grow together and make travel and tourism safe, secure, productive, enjoyable and economical.

JACKSON HOSPITALITY SERVICES: CASE STUDY OF A COMPANY

The success of JHS lies in part with its seasoned management. Led by Founder and Chairman Cory Jackson, Sr. and supported by sons Cory Jr. and Neal, JHS is a team of experienced hotel professionals dedicated to providing excellent management for the properties that the company services.

1970s: Company Beginnings

JHS was originally founded by Cory Jackson, Sr., in 1977 as Jackson Motel Management Company. The roots of hospitality run deep in the Jackson family. Immediately after the Korean War, Mr. Jackson's father had the vision to develop a new motor hotel along busy highway 78 on the eastern side of Birmingham. The neat white motel soon developed a reputation for cleanliness and service that turned Motel Birmingham into an Alabama landmark.

Having worked in all aspects of the family operation, Cory Sr. had his first taste of hotel management at the Motel Birmingham. A mortgage banker by trade, Mr. Jackson would found Jackson Motel Management when the family's mortgage banking business was sold in the late 1970s.

Mr. Jackson would go on to develop and manage several Sheraton and Holiday Inn properties in the Birmingham area during the 1970s, including the wildly successful Sheraton Mountain Brook Inn.

1980s: Steady Growth—Key West Inns are Born

Jackson motel management grew steadily through the decade of the eighties, developing and operating many successful properties, including the landmark Sheraton Perimeter Park South in Birmingham and the Sheraton Capstone in Tuscaloosa.

Jackson became involved in franchising during the mid-1980s, seeing the need for smaller hotels in niche markets around the Southeast. The chain, Key West Inns, has developed into a solid regional chain under Jackson's leadership.

1990s: Name Change Reflects Positioning

In 1991, Jackson Motel Management Company became Jackson Hospitality Services, better representing the company's general focus as it developed into a major national hotel management company.

Now in its fourth decade, JHS growth and opportunities continue, allowing the company to marshall an ever-increasing resource of talent and experience to service its current and expanding portfolio.

Jackson Hospitality Services management staff, at both the corporate and property levels, actively support and participate in numerous professional lodging organizations. JHS Hospitality Industry Memberships are often in leadership positions.

Hotel Management and Development Services

Hotel Management Strategies: Even the Odds

Success in the hospitality industry is defined in many different ways. For Jackson Hospitality Services, that definition lies in providing return on investment and increasing asset value for its clients.

Achieving this level of success involves many factors. JHS provides proactive management of those factors implemented through the following programmes that are consistently applied at each managed property:

Do I Need a Hotel Management Company?

It is one of the most important decisions that any hotel owner has to make. Should they run their hotel themselves or through their own organization, or should they employ the services of a professional hotel management company? The answer to the question lies in the experience level and amount of time that can be allotted to the management of the property.

No Room for Error

In the highly complex world of the hotel business today, there is no room for error. Competition is fierce. Costs are rising. Recruiting and retaining quality employees is harder than ever. There are literally hundreds of critical decisions and details that have to be attended to in a successful operation each and every day. Sales and marketing decisions. Human resource issues. Operational questions. Franchise rules. Accounting problems. These details and decisions take lots of time and thought.

Time is money. As a full-service Hotel Management Company, Jackson Hospitality Services leverages time for hotel owners by taking care of the day-to-day details of management at their hotels. This allows them to concentrate on the things that are more important in their lives.

Additionally, many of the decisions have expensive repercussions if they are not made correctly. Since 1977, Jackson Hospitality Services' seasoned experience has provided the peace of mind that our client hotel owners need about their hotel investment decisions. We currently manage 34 hotels.

Our mission is to maximize the return on investment for our client hotel investments through professional leadership, solid operations, aggressive sales and marketing, content and well-trained employees delivering excellent guest service, back-to-basics operations and timely financial information.

The Stakes are High—Even the Odds

If the answer to the above question is "Yes" or even "Maybe", give us a call and let's talk about what Jackson Hospitality Services can do for you as a hotel owner to not only even the odds, but stack them in your favour for a profitable hotel operation.

Turn Key Hotel Consulting, Development and Management Services:

- Hotel development and pre-opening services.
- Cost control, budgeting and financial performance review.
- Hotel sales planning and marketing.
- Franchise relations and inspections.
- Hospitality employee recruiting, training and relations.
- Complete accounting and reporting services.
- Capital expenditure planning.
- Hotel renovation project management.
- Asset management for financial institutions.

Hotel Sales and Marketing Services

Planning and Establishing Hotel Revenue Goals

A good marketing plan is like a trusty road map. It tells us where we're going, how to get there and, most importantly, lets us know we're there when we're there. Long-range thinking is more than just going through the motions. A hotel sales department requires a vehicle that will enable it to fulfill its overall business objectives.

The Annual Market Plan is the sales department's strategy to achieve the desired results, including hotel revenue management. This report includes a market segment analysis that constitutes the hotel's business objectives... a means of deciding the direction of the hotel and sales department within the framework of the objectives of the Franchise Company and Jackson Hospitality Services.

JHS Marketing Plan Process

- A strategic Sales and Marketing Plan is created each year for each JHS property.
- The tactical initiatives of this plan (Sales Action Plan) are reviewed monthly to ensure property compliance.

- The plan is also reviewed each month between the Director of Operations and the General Manager to determine any new approaches that could better market the hotel.
- JHS monitors coordination between property and franchiser marketing (*i.e.* Choice, Hilton, Hampton, Sheraton), ensuring that properties capitalize on all marketing opportunities and support provided by their franchiser.

Hotel Internet Marketing Strategies

Business generated from the Internet is rapidly on the increase. In 2004, 16 per cent of all revenues in hospitality will be generated from the Internet (14% in 2003). By 2006, the Internet will contribute over 24 per cent of all hotel bookings (CSFB). This year 54 per cent of all Internet bookings in hospitality will be direct-to-consumer (*i.e.*, via hotel-owned web sites). Some major brands (*e.g.* Marriott, Hilton) and proactive hotels and resorts already enjoy Direct vs. Indirect online distribution ratios of 75 : 25. Direct online distribution cuts costs (such as brochures), attracts affluent customers and lessens the dependency on online discounters and more traditional and expensive channels.

Whether you are an independent or branded hotel, a major hotel chain or hotel management company, you can stay ahead of your competitors and capture new market share with an effective Direct Online Distribution Strategy. The center-point of this strategy is the development of the hotel's own website, in addition to their franchise web-presence (if any).

As part of your comprehensive total online distribution strategy, JHS can assist in:

- Evaluating the overall use of the Internet as a hotel marketing tool.
- Development and deployment of the hotel website.
- Perform a website Optimization Strategy to make your existing hotel website user-friendly, search engine-friendly and travel booker-friendly.

- Perform a robust Search Engine Strategy designed to improve your website positioning on search engines in order to boost direct consumer bookings.

85 per cent of Internet users rely on search engines to locate information on the Web and that search patterns for accommodations are strictly destination-focused.

Hotel Development and Pre-Opening Services

Hotels are different from other types of real estate investments primarily due to their daily occupancy and revenue fluctuations, the requirement for specialized management, and labour intensity. Understanding the cyclical nature and dynamics of hotel markets are critical to good investment decision-making. An initial analysis of market and financial feasibility is perhaps the most important aspect in hotel investment decision-making.

Our hotel consulting staff has years of experience in hotel development and operations management. The hotel consulting services we provide are unique for each project we undertake, and are therefore tailored to meet each client's individual needs. Our experience makes us ideally suited to assist you with your hotel development project, from feasibility study to pre-opening and opening.

Feasibility Assistance

- Analyze and verify feasibility studies.
- Assist in site selection and evaluation.
- Coordinate hotel demand studies.
- Prepare financial proforma.
- Prepare preliminary construction and related cost estimate.

Planning/Design

- Coordinate hotel room design and food and beverage areas.

- Coordinate architect, engineer, land planner, and/or interior designer.
- Coordinate layout/procurement of hotel furnishing, kitchen and lounge equipment, laundry equipment, and commercial area furnishings.
- Coordinate all computerized areas—front desk, energy management, restaurant and administration.
- Coordinate the telephone system, key and lock system, and audio-visual system.
- Specify/procure ice machines, vacuum cleaners, maid carts, etc.

Interior Design Assistance

- Interview and recommend a design firm.
- Assist the interior design firm with the furnishing specifications:
    - lobby, corridors and meeting rooms and
    - rooms restaurant and lounge.

Construction Project Management

- Function as project manager (fee basis).
- Act as general contractor (fee basis).
- Coordinate input with architect, engineer, etc.
- Consult with owner on bids, changes and/or selecting general contractor.
- Take bids on project.
- Perform pre-opening inspections and punch list for hotel.

Pre-opening Services

- Create and implement the pre-opening marketing plan.
- Assemble pre-opening budgets (working capital, food, beverage, linens, china, etc.).
- Recruit, interview, and hire all key management and sales personnel.

- Train all key personnel.
- Recommend advertising agency.
- Establish definitive objectives and action plans for all departments.
- Obtain business licenses.
- Develop pricing for rooms, food and beverage.
- Develop specifications and bids on building insurance.
- Coordinate the procurement of guest supplies and employee uniforms.
- Interface with potential hotel concessionaires.
- Develop employee benefit programme and policy manual.

Hotel Cost Control and Financial Review

Charting a Course to Success with Effective Cost Controls

Years of hotel management experience has taught us what revenue and expense items to track. These are important distinctions when operating a hotel in the real world, where the goal is to meet and exceed profit targets. Our information gathering and reporting systems are designed to provide efficient use of hotel staff and technology-and to insure that JHS has the necessary operational statistics and details to provide cost-control oversight.

Detailed operating budgets are used to carefully control spending because good control on expenses is critical to achieving excellent operating margins. JHS implements and monitors strong internal controls which are critical to preventing losses through fraud and theft. We ensure that accepted risk management practices are being followed in order to reduce exposure.

All of this is designed to maximize the potential of your property by producing the best possible bottom line and increasing its eventual sales value.

- Each JHS property operates under an annual budget that is prepared in advance.

- The budget is submitted to ownership for review and approval.
- All financial performance is measured against this plan.
- All financial statements are reviewed by the Director of Operations and a summary is prepared and reviewed by JHS Executive Management.
- Monthly meetings with ownership.

Adherence to Franchise Requirements

Building a Solid Relationship with Your Franchise Company

JHS has tremendous insight into working with hotel franchise companies. We have excellent relationships with nearly every major brand, having developed and operated hotels under many franchise flags during our years in business.

Let us take away your headaches in franchise selection or brand compliance. Our Operations Staff regularly monitors each property's condition in light of their specific franchise requirements regarding operations, audits and marketing opportunities.

Franchise-Related Services

- Franchise hotel management.
- Assistance in Franchise selection and contract negotiation.
- JHS ensures that each managed property operates according to the requirements of its franchise agreement through property visits and mock inspections.
- JHS has Directors of Operations with specific training and experience for most major franchises (Choice, Hampton, Holiday Inn, Sheraton).
- JHS staff keeps abreast of all the latest marketing strategies of all major franchises so that opportunities are not missed.

Hotel Human Resources Management

Managing people is one of the most critical aspects of successfully operating a hotel. Payroll and related costs account for a large percentage of overall cost, making their effective management critical.

JHS abides by a philosophy that honours the employee through effective communication, proactive employee programmes, training, and benefit programmes. JHS properties operate under a set of Human Resource Guidelines that provide the proper steps for the management of employees.

JHS can Assist in all Areas Related to Human Resources

- Employee Handbook Creation and Review.
- Insure proper hiring and training process conforms with all Franchise and Government requirements (including immigration issues).
- Manage benefits programmes; provide most cost-effective providers.
- Provide human resources support at the property.
- Create, monitor and implement hotel employee incentive programmes.
- Monitor payroll costs directly associated with room sales (*i.e.*, housekeeping, front desk) closely to insure that it conforms with quality and cost standards.
- JHS is an Equal Opportunity employer.

Hotel Accounting and Reporting Services

Jackson Hospitality Services offers full service accounting to all of its client hotels. JHS has an Accounting Department staffed to handle accounts payable, financial reporting and other services for the companies managed properties.

Accounting processes are regularly analyzed by ownership's CPA firms. Some larger properties have their accounting performed on-site. JHS coordinates the set-up of the accounting systems and monitors them on a consistent basis.

JHS Accounting Services Include

- Sophisticated "Microsoft Dynamics GP (Formerly Great Plains)" accounting software, with reporting capability for all common reporting requirements.
- Reports include:
    - Disbursement activity.
    - Accounts payables.
    - Accounts receivables.
    - Changes in cash position.
    - General ledger transactions.
    - Balance sheets.
    - Hotel financial statements.

Hotel Capital Management and Planning Services

The selection of effective capital expenditures is critical to the short and long-term value of the hotel. Strategic planning is needed to insure that cash reserves will be sufficient when the required improvements are required. Short and long-term planning is needed to insure that cash reserves will be sufficient to meet the cost of improvements to be made, as scheduled, to maintain (and enhance) the value of the hotel.

JHS will work effectively with the owner to establish the amount of reserves that should be set-aside for capital expenditure on an ongoing basis. While a general rule of thumb for the level of repairs and maintenance, is approximately 3-4 per cent of hotel's revenue, this amount can vary with the age of the property, and declining revenue levels.

Annual Planning

Each year, JHS updates a short-term and long-term capital plan for each of our client hotels. A complete report is presented to ownership for assistance in assessing upcoming capital improvement planning. This ensures that you, as the owner, are not faced with unexpected capital expenditures.

Hotel Renovation Management Services

Is your hotel "behind the curve" regarding amenities and services that are now expected to support top rates? Are you losing business because of external corridors or inadequate safety features? Does a change in Franchise affiliation require major physical changes?

According to Price Waterhouse Coopers, increased revenues for 2004 are supporting hotel owners and management companies plans to return to approximately 1998 levels for capital expenditures.

Among the changes in guestroom and hotel design that are driving many renovations:

- ❖ Better beds and bedding, in both comfort and quality of material.
- ❖ Televisions set atop low-lying dresser drawers or cabinets.
- ❖ Traditional armoire or televisions mounted on the walls of hotel rooms to take advantage of their space-saving design.
- ❖ Adoption of local themes in exterior architecture, public space décor and restaurant themes (particularly in the upscale and upper-upscale hotels).
- ❖ High speed Internet access based on comments from an increasing number of guests expressing this as an important amenity.
- ❖ Electronic "function boards" and directories and generally better signage.

Whatever, your property's needs, JHS is ready to assist in planning and implementation of your hotel renovation project.

Hotel Asset Management Services

To succeed in an ever competitive market, a hotel must be able to identify and act on the characteristics and needs that make it different from other hotels. It is necessary to identify its strengths and weaknesses, and the ever-changing challenges in order to maximize owner return.

At JHS, we can focus on the smallest details of a hotel's operation and bring improvement to that area. We can analyze every aspect of your building and operation to find areas for strengthening and improvement in all operated and non-operated departments.

Improving Both Top and Bottom-Line Results

The hospitality professionals at JHS will always keep sight of the mission to optimize asset value through well-refined operations. We can improve hotel performance at the top line and at the bottom line. We will work closely with your sales department to demonstrate ways to improve revenue/top line results. Likewise, we identify uncontrolled expenses and show you where money is unnecessarily flowing out of your property, negatively impacting the bottom line.

Optimizing Your Property Value

JHS provides quality asset management services, drawing on years of operating experience on behalf of a variety of owners and ownership groups. Our combination of hotel analytical knowledge and extensive operational experience provide us with the experience required to develop the strategies and management practices that will result in increased cash flow and asset value.

We have complete expertise in all areas of hotel operations and can assist in evaluating entire properties or specific divisions. We then provide specific recommendations and strategies to enhance the operation.

Hoteliers International

Hoteliers International Corporation—Experienced Professional Hotel Managers, Hotel Management and Hotel Consulting Services—Hotel Consultants and Hotel Managers in the Global Marketplace. Let us help you to attain, or restore, achievable returns and maximise revenues and capital growth for your hotel systems and resort assets.

The service that we offer today is the focus of everything we invest in for tomorrow.

Alan Johnson, President & CEO

Hoteliers International Corporation provides consulting services to the hospitality industry.

Hoteliers International Corporation is a long experienced hotel management and hotel consulting company servicing all areas of the hospitality industry. We help you by offering a "one-stop" complete hotel consultant and management service for hotel, resort property, serviced apartments, a diverse array of hospitality assets as well as building and design services. Let us help establish, or rebuild, hotel profitability, solve hospitality management systems inefficiencies, re-engineer hotel staff and management policies and guest programmes, establish effective marketing programmes and manage your new developments from start to the first guest registration and beyond.

Given our experience with hotel and resort properties, Hoteliers International can provide the link between owners of properties, and the consumer as guest, to provide services at an affordable rate while ensuring a good and improving return to hotel stakeholders.

Hoteliers International, led by President and CEO, Alan Johnson, can establish or rebuild profitability in hotel and resort properties by exercising management control, direction and measurement to restore achievable returns and to maximize value added assets by revenue and capital growth.

Hoteliers International can further enhance the profitability and momentum of hotel and resort properties by value-adding assets through marketing and advertising initiatives and further investment in maintenance and upgrading, all while maintaining cost and expense control.

"Our company will remain alert to global developments in hospitality services and be positioned to maximize opportunities as they arise."

A well-respected team of sales and marketing professionals develop and maintain connections with major airlines, travel agencies, wholesale tour operators and government sponsored marketing agencies in Australia and throughout the world to assure client's success.

The Company

Hoteliers International Corporation is an experienced award winning management company servicing all areas of the hospitality industry, including hotels and serviced apartments.

Hoteliers International can provide the link between owners of properties and the consumer as guest to provide services at an affordable rate while ensuring maximized return to stakeholders.

President and CEO, Alan Johnson CHA, states, "Hoteliers International, can establish or rebuild profitability in properties by exercising management control, establishing direction and developing measurement standards."

Through marketing and advertising, maintenance and upgrading, Hoteliers International can further enhance profitability while controlling costs and expenses.

Protect Your Investment

Let Hoteliers International's award winning consultants:

- Establish or rebuild profitability,
- Solve management systems inefficiencies,
- Re-engineer policies and guest programmes,
- Establish effective marketing programmes or
- Manage your new developments.

Hoteliers International Corporation is also Australia's leading hotel management company. Since the 1970's Hoteliers International has owned, operated and consulted with numerous hotels and tourism associated properties throughout Australia, the Pacific Rim and the USA.

Through continued diversification, Hoteliers International is committed to remaining at the forefront of the hospitality industry.

HOTELIER: A UNIQUE CASE STUDY

Hotelier is a South Korean drama broadcast by MBC in 2001. Hotelier contains a total of 20 episodes. The word "Hotelier" literally means "a person who owns or runs a hotel. The drama was set in Seoul Hotel, a five-star hotel which embarked on expensive, construction upgrading.

Synopsis

President Choi, hotelier of Seoul hotel, died from a heart attack hours after Kim Bok-man, his old friend informed him of serious plans his company, Hankang Distribution, to buy over shares of Seoul hotel. He was succeeded by his wife, Yon Bong-sook, who had never assumed any positions in the past to run the hotel. The reason for Yun assuming the position was to carry on the works of her late husband. Her son, Choi Young-jae, was a dissolute man who refused to work and was capable of taking drugs.

Yun was confronted by pressures from Kim, who was making his way to buy up Seoul Hotel's shares. To fend off the competitor, Yun sends one of the hotel managers, Suh Jin Young, to America and try to rehire Seoul Hotel's former Head Manager, Han Tae-Jun, who was forced to resign after a scandal involving the hotel. Han was taking care of a drug-addict, dissolute Korean-American girl who was nearly forced to take drugs.

Kim was looking forward to make his attack and hired Attorney Frank Shin Dong-Hyuk, a wealthy Korean-American takeover businessman, to assist him in buying over the hotel's shares through various means.

Frank Shin agrees to the job only after meeting Suh Jin Young when she travels to America (to find Han) and learns that she actually works at this "Seoul Hotel" of Bok-Man's proposal. Travelling to Seoul Korea for the first time since when he left as a child, Frank and his loyal business assistant Leo move into a "Seoul Hotel" chalet to purportedly conduct their secret business with Bok-Man.

Kim learnt of Seoul Hotel's mismanagement through Frank Shin's infiltration as a double-agent. Whilst carrying out his duties, Frank found himself in love with Suh. Suh was later torn between relations with Frank and Han.

Choi Young Jae fell in love with Kim Yun-Hee, the daughter of Hankang Distribution's manager Kim Bok-man, during a nightclub meeting. However, relations went downhill as Kim developed a crush in a birthday party held at Seoul Hotel.

Han was weighed with duties of defending the hotel from their competitors at the same time protecting Kim from her abusive father and Suh from falling in love with Frank. Han was also weighed with the other duty of mending the ways of the previously dissolute Choi.

Frank soon discovered his dissolute sister, whom Han had taken care of. They went to meet their father, who called them by their Korean names, Dong-hyuk and Dong-hee. Frank's attitude changed as he switched sides to helping Seoul Hotel.

Han and Frank eventually re-established Seoul Hotel's position, but Yun was diagnosed with cancer. Frank and Suh were married; Han and Kim later married and Han, Frank and the younger Choi became cooperate partners in running the hotel.

ACCESS HOTEL MANAGEMENT: AN OVERVIEW

Rarely does a hotel management company take a hands-on approach in such diverse areas as property operations, customer relationship management, direct sales management, and human resource development. Access Hotel Management, however, takes pride in our expertise in these functions as well as a number of others that affect the customer experience and owner profitability. With extensive backgrounds in hospitality marketing and years of direct experience in the hotel and resort industry, our company's top executives are uniquely qualified to help each property gain exposure and achieve the ultimate in guest service and market penetration.

Utilizing time-tested and proven strategies developed through years of service as Operators and Corporate officers,

Access offers a diverse selection of services to asset owners, including:

- ❖ Property Management,
- ❖ Asset Management,
- ❖ Acquisition,
- ❖ Investment Return Analysis,
- ❖ Asset Disposition,
- ❖ Sales and Marketing, and
- ❖ Technology Consulting.

Access Hotel Management staff offers a broad range of expertise with nearly 60 years of combined hospitality-related experience in such areas as hotel and resort operations, development, finance, food and beverage, consulting, and management/franchise contract negotiation.

Complete Hotel Management Services

Our management expertise spans the full spectrum of the services required to develop and operate a successful hotel.

- ❖ *Operations*: Guest services, house-keeping, maintenance, back office...
- ❖ *Financials:* Centralized accounting, immediate reports, local control...
- ❖ *Marketing and Sales*: Brand strategies, local marketing, Internet marketing...
- ❖ *Food and Beverage:* Restaurant, banquets, room service, special events...
- ❖ *Development and Construction*: New construction, renovations, repairs, additions...

We Maximize Your ROI

When you trust your hotel to Access, we will dedicate ourselves to achieving your goals and running a highly efficient and effective hotel. You can expect:

- *A custom contract meeting your unique needs*: Short or long term, financing assistance, and more.
- *High returns on your investment*: We typically exceed our peer group in returns—why settle for average returns.
- *A hotel you will be proud to own*: Smoothly-running, tight operations and exceeding Brand requirements.

Operational, Financial and Facility Assessments

Before a course of action can be determined, asset managers must first know what they have and what the options are. Access can assist you by providing the following:

Property Assessment

- Basic information about the condition of the physical plant.
- Local market conditions.
- Assess and compare the subject property to its competitors.
- Operational Review.

A Review of Operating Procedures, Systems and Controls

- Staffing and operating policies,
- Management effectiveness,
- Quality of product and service,
- An opinion of strength of senior management, and
- Financial Review (Remote and/or Onsite).

Financial Statements, Records and Reports

- Cash control methods,
- Operating ratios,
- Sources of data and financial process,
- Line-by-line Profit and Loss assessment against industry, and standards.

'The Creation and Enhancement of Property and Business Values for The Owner'

Our Asset Management Team concentrates on reviewing property operations and capital expenditures; identifying opportunities to increase profitability; ensuring competitiveness in procurement; ensuring the hotel operator is focused on the critical elements of success; monitoring changes in the competition and reacting accordingly; and analyzing results on behalf of ownership.

We will specifically provide the following:

- ❖ Maximize property returns through the pursuit of strategies for value creation.
- ❖ Review and analyze monthly operator performance.
- ❖ Participate in planning and monitoring of capital projects.
- ❖ Administer owner relations and represent the company at board meetings.
- ❖ Review and critique annual marketing plans and budgets.
- ❖ Review asset positioning and make comparisons to market competitors.
- ❖ Assemble and evaluate pertinent market and economic data.
- ❖ Assist with legal issues and contract compliance.
- ❖ Preparations of financial projections and valuations.
- ❖ Prepare quarterly investment performance report.
- ❖ Administer legal, tax and accounting formalities for each property.

Chapter 3

Hotel Marketing, Sales and Consulting: Selected Case Studies

HOTEL MARKETING

Marketing is a societal process which discerns consumers' wants, focusing on a product or service to fulfill those wants, attempting to move the consumers toward the products or services offered. Marketing is fundamental to any businesses growth. The marketing teams (marketers) are tasked to create consumer awareness of the products or services through marketing techniques. Unless it pays due attention to its products and services and consumers' demographics and desires, a business will not usually prosper over time.

Marketing tends to be seen as a creative industry, which includes advertising, distribution and selling. It is also concerned with anticipating the customers' future needs and wants, which are often discovered through market research.

Essentially, marketing is the process of creating or directing an organization to be successful in selling a product or service that people not only desire, but are willing to buy.

Therefore, good marketing must be able to create a "proposition" or set of benefits for the end customer that delivers value through products or services.

Its specialist areas include:

- Advertising and branding,
- Direct marketing,
- International marketing,

- Public relations,
- Communications,
- Strategic management,
- Market research,
- Events organization,
- Database marketing, and
- Search engine marketing.

A market-focused, or customer-focused, organization first determines what its potential customers desire, and then builds the product or service. Marketing theory and practice is justified in the belief that customers use a product or service because they have a need, or because it provides a perceived benefit.

Two major factors of marketing are the recruitment of new customers (acquisition) and the retention and expansion of relationships with existing customers (base management). Once a marketer has converted the prospective buyer, base management marketing takes over. The process for base management shifts the marketer to building a relationship, nurturing the links, enhancing the benefits that sold the buyer in the first place, and improving the product/service continuously to protect the business from competitive encroachments.

For a marketing plan to be successful, the mix of the four "Ps" must reflect the wants and desires of the consumers or Shoppers in the target market. Trying to convince a market segment to buy something they don't want is extremely expensive and seldom successful. Marketers depend on insights from marketing research, both formal and informal, to determine what consumers want and what they are willing to pay for. Marketers hope that this process will give them a sustainable competitive advantage. Marketing management is the practical application of this process. The offer is also an important addition to the 4P's theory.

Within most organizations, the activities encompassed by the marketing function are led by a Vice-President or Director of Marketing. A growing number of organizations, especially large US companies, have a Chief Marketing Officer position, reporting to the Chief Executive Officer.

The American Marketing Association (AMA) states, "Marketing is an organizational function and a set of processes for creating, communicating and delivering value to customers and for managing customer relationships in ways that benefit the organization and its stakeholders."

Marketing methods are informed by many of the social sciences, particularly psychology, sociology, and economics. Anthropology is also a small, but growing influence. Market research underpins these activities. Through advertising, it is also related to many of the creative arts. Marketing is a wide and heavily interconnected subject with extensive publications. It is also an area of activity infamous for re-inventing itself and its vocabulary according to the times and the culture.

Two Levels of Marketing

- *Strategic marketing* attempts to determine how an organization competes against its competitors in a market place. In particular, it aims at generating a competitive advantage relative to its competitors.
- *Operational marketing* executes marketing functions to attract and keep customers and to maximize the value derived for them, as well as to satisfy the customer with prompt services and meeting the customer expectations. Operational Marketing includes the determination of the marketing mix (4 Ps).

Four Ps

In the early 1960's, Professor Neil Borden at Harvard Business School identified a number of company performance actions that can influence the consumer decision to purchase goods or services. Borden suggested that all those actions of the company represented a "Marketing Mix". Professor E. Jerome McCarthy, also at the Harvard Business School in the early 1960s, suggested that the Marketing Mix contained 4 elements: product, price, place and promotion.

In popular usage, "marketing" is the promotion of products, especially advertising and branding. However, in professional usage the term has a wider meaning which recognizes that marketing is customer-centered. Products are often developed to meet the desires of groups of customers or even, in some cases, for specific customers. E. Jerome McCarthy divided marketing into four general sets of activities. His typology has become so universally recognized that his four activity sets, the Four Ps, have passed into the language.

The Four Ps are:

- *Product*: The product aspects of marketing deal with the specifications of the actual goods or services, and how it relates to the end-user's needs and wants. The scope of a product generally includes supporting elements such as warranties, guarantees and support.
- *Pricing*: This refers to the process of setting a price for a product, including discounts. The price need not be monetary—it can simply be what is exchanged for the product or services, *e.g.*, time, energy, psychology or attention.
- *Promotion*: This includes advertising, sales promotion, publicity, and personal selling, branding and refers to the various methods of promoting the product, brand, or company.
- *Placement* (*or distribution*): Refers to how the product gets to the customer; for example, point of sale placement or retailing. This fourth P has also sometimes been called *Place,* referring to the channel by which a product or services is sold (*e.g.* online vs. retail), which geographic region or industry, to which segment (young adults, families, business people), etc.

These four elements are often referred to as the marketing mix, which a marketer can use to craft a marketing plan. The four Ps model is most useful when marketing low value consumer products. Industrial products, services, high value consumer products require adjustments to this model. Services marketing must account for the unique nature of services. Industrial or B2B marketing must account for the long-term contractual agreements that are typical in supply chain transactions. Relationship marketing attempts to do this by looking at marketing from a long-term relationship perspective rather than individual transactions.

As a counter to this, Morgan, in *Riding the Waves of Change* (Jossey-Bass, 1988), suggests that one of the greatest limitations of the 4 Ps approach "is that it unconsciously emphasizes the inside-out view (looking from the company outwards), whereas the essence of marketing should be the outside—in approach". Nevertheless, the 4 Ps offer a memorable and workable guide to the major categories of marketing activity, as well as a framework within which these can be used.

Seven Ps

As well as the standard four P's (product, pricing, promotion and place), services marketing calls upon an extra three, totaling seven and known together as the extended marketing mix. These are:

- *People*: Any person coming into contact with customers can have an impact on overall satisfaction. Whether as part of a supporting service to a product or involved in a total service, people are particularly important because, in the customer's eyes, they are generally inseparable from the total service. As a result of this, they must be appropriately trained, well-motivated and the right type of person. Fellow customers are also sometimes referred to under 'people', as they too can affect the customer's service experience, (*e.g.*, at a sporting event).
- *Process*: This is the process(es) involved in providing a service and the behaviour of people, which can be crucial to customer satisfaction.
- *Physical evidence*: Unlike a product, a service cannot be experienced before it is delivered, which makes it intangible. This, therefore, means that potential customers could perceive greater risk when deciding whether to use a service. To reduce the feeling of risk, thus improving the chance for success, it is often vital to offer potential customers the chance to see what a service would be like. This is done by providing physical

evidence, such as case studies, testimonials or demonstrations.

Web 2.0 and Marketing New 4Ps

The original 4Ps concept idea was developed to help marketers manage the four most important aspect of marketing. With the Internet and the Web 2.0, marketers have needed to adapt a broader perspective on these elements. Idris Mootee devised a "New 4Ps" model in 2001 to supplement the traditional marketing 4Ps. They are personalization, participation, peer-to-peer and perdictive modelling:

- *Personalization:* It is here referred customization of products and services through the use of the Internet. Early examples include—Dell on-line and Amazon.com, but this concept is further extended with emerging social media and advanced algorithms. Emerging technologies will continue to push this idea forward.
- *Participation:* This is to allow customer to participate in what the brand should stand for; what should be the product directions and even which ads to run. This concept is laying the foundation for disruptive change through democratization of information.
- *Peer-to-Peer:* This refers to customer networks and communities where advocacy happens. The historical problem with marketing is that it is "interruptive" in nature, trying to impose a brand on the customer. This is most apparent in TV advertising. These "passive customer bases" will ultimately be replaced by the "active customer communities". Brand engagement happens within those conversations. P2P is now being referred as Social Computing and is likely to be the most disruptive force in the future of marketing.
- *Predictive modelling:* This refers to predictive algorithms, such as neural network, that are being successfully applied in marketing problems (both a regression as well as a classification problem).

Product

Scope

- *Breadth*—Number of product lines in a range.
- *Depth*—Number of product items in a product line.

Steps in Product Design

- Design and development of product ideas.
- Selection of and sifting through product ideas.
- Design and testing of product concept.
- Analysis of instead of product concept.
- Design and testing of emotional product.

Packaging and Trademarks

Requirements of Good Packaging

- Appropriately designed for target market.
- Eye-catching (particularly for retail/consumer sales) .
- Suitable to product.
- Compliant with retailers' requirements.
- Promotes image of enterprise.
- Distinguishable from competitors' products.
- Strong, convenient, well-designed.
- Point of difference in service and supply of product.

Forms of Packaging

- *Specialty packaging*: Emphasizes the elegant character of the product.
- *Packaging for double-use.*
- *Combination packaging* two or more products packaged in the same container.
- *Kaleidoscopic packaging*: Packaging changes continually to reflect a series or particular theme.

- *Packaging for immediate consumption*: To be thrown away after use.
- *Packaging for resale*: Packed, into appropriate quantities, for the retailer or wholesaler.

Significance of a Trademark

- Distinguishes one company's goods from those of another.
- Serves as advertisement for quality.
- Protects both consumers and manufacturers.
- Used in displays and advertising campaigns.
- Used to market new products.

Requirements of a Good Trademark

- Reflects products' advantages.
- Good, simple language.
- Easily pronounced and remembered.
- Distinct from names of other products.
- Easily added to an existing range.
- Easily registered for legal protection.

Pricing

Pricing refers to the amount of money exchanged for a product. This value is determined by utility to the consumer in terms of money and/or sacrifice that he is prepared to give for it.

Objectives

- Definite sales volume,
- Achieve profit,
- Larger market share,
- Maintain market share,
- Eliminate competition,
- Advantages of mass production, and

- Satisfactory return on capital.

Factors Influencing Price-Determination

- Production and distribution costs,
- Substitute goods available,
- Normal trade practices,
- Fixed prices,
- Reaction of distributors,
- Reaction of consumers, and
- Nature of demand.
    - Elastic
    - Inelastic
    - Form of market:
        - Perfect competition
        - Monopolistic competition
        - Monopoly
        - Oligopoly
        - Philosophy.

Steps to Determine Price

- Determine market share to be captured,
- Set-up price strategy,
- Estimate demand,
- Evaluate competitors' reactions.

Distribution

Channels

- Manufacturer to consumer (most direct) .
- Manufacturer to wholesaler to retailer to consumer (traditional) .
- Manufacturer to agent to retailer to consumer (current).

- ❖ Manufacturer to agent to wholesaler to retailer to consumer.
- ❖ Manufacturer to agent to customer (ex: AMWAY).

Manufacturers

Reasons for Direct Selling Methods

- ❖ Manufacturer wants to demonstrate goods.
- ❖ Wholesalers, retailers and agents not actively selling.
- ❖ Manufacturer unable to convince wholesalers or retailers to stock product.
- ❖ High profit margin added to goods by wholesalers and retailers.
- ❖ Middlemen unable to transport.

Reasons for Indirect Selling Methods

- ❖ Manufacturer does not have the financial resources to distribute goods.
- ❖ Distribution channels already established.
- ❖ Manufacturer has no knowledge of efficient distribution.
- ❖ Manufacturer wishes to use capital for further production.
- ❖ Too many consumers in a large area; difficult to reach.
- ❖ Manufacturer does not have a wide assortment of goods to enable efficient marketing.

Wholesalers

Reasons for Using Wholesalers

- ❖ Bear risk of selling goods to retailer or consumer,
- ❖ Storage space,
- ❖ Decrease transport costs,
- ❖ Grant credit to retailers,
- ❖ Able to sell for the manufacturers,
- ❖ Give advice to manufacturers,
- ❖ Break down products into smaller quantities.

Reasons for Bypassing Wholesalers

- Limited storage facilities,
- Retailers' preferences,
- Wholesaler cannot promote products successfully,
- Development of wholesalers' own brands,
- Desire for closer market contact,
- Position of power,
- Cost of wholesalers' services,
- Price stabilisation,
- Need for rapid distribution,
- Make more money.

Ways of Bypassing Wholesalers

- Sales offices or branches
- Mail orders,
- Direct sales to retailers,
- Travelling agents, and
- Direct Orders.

Agents

- *Commission agents* work for anyone who needs their services. They do not acquire ownership of goods but receive *del credere* commission.
- *Selling agents* act on an extended contractual basis, selling all of the products of the manufacturer. They have full authority regarding price and terms of sale.
- *Buying agents* buy goods on behalf of producers and retailers. They have an expert knowledge of the purchasing function.
- *Brokers* specialize in the sale of one specific product. They receive a brokerage.
- *Factory representatives* represent more than one manufacturer. They operate within a specific area and sell

related lines of goods but have limited authority regarding price and sales terms.

Marketing Communications

Marketing communications breaks down the strategies involved with marketing messages into categories based on the goals of each message. There are distinct stages in converting strangers to customers that govern the communication medium that should be used.

Advertising

- ❖ Paid form of public presentation and expressive promotion of ideas.
- ❖ Aimed at masses.
- ❖ Manufacturer may determine what goes into advertisement.
- ❖ Pervasive and impersonal medium.

Functions and Advantages of Successful Advertising

- ❖ Task of the salesman made easier.
- ❖ Forces manufacturer to live up to conveyed image.
- ❖ Protects and warns customers against false claims and inferior products.
- ❖ Enables manufacturer to mass-produce product.
- ❖ Continuous reminder.
- ❖ Uninterrupted production a possibility.
- ❖ Increases goodwill.
- ❖ Raises standards of living (or perceptions thereof).
- ❖ Prices decrease with increased popularity.
- ❖ Educates manufacturer and wholesaler about competitors' offerings as well as shortcomings in their own.

Objectives

- ❖ Maintain demand for well-known goods.

- Introduce new and unknown goods.
- Increase demand for well-known goods.

Requirements of a Good Advertisement

- Attract attention.
- Stimulate interest.
- Create a desire.
- Bring about action.
- Create Awareness.

Eight Steps in an Advertising Campaign

- Market research.
- Setting out aims.
- Budgeting.
- Choice of media (TV, newspaper and radio).
- Choice of actors (New Trend).
- Design and wording.
- Coordination.
- Test results.

Personal Sales

Oral presentation given by a salesman who approaches individuals or a group of potential customers:

- Live, interactive relationship.
- Personal interest.
- Attention and response.
- Interesting presentation.

Sales Promotion

Short-term incentives to encourage buying of products:

- Instant appeal.
- Anxiety to sell.

Marketing Public Relations (MPR)

Stimulation of demand through press release giving a favourable report to a product:

- Higher degree of credibility.
- Effectively news.
- Boosts enterprise's image.

Customer Focus

Many companies today have a customer focus (or customer orientation). This implies that the company focuses its activities and products on consumer demands. Generally there are three ways of doing this: the customer-driven approach, the sense of identifying market changes and the product innovation approach.

In the consumer-driven approach, consumer wants are the drivers of all strategic marketing decisions. No strategy is pursued until it passes the test of consumer research. Every aspect of a market offering, including the nature of the product itself, is driven by the needs of potential consumers. The starting point is always the consumer. The rationale for this approach is that there is no point spending R&D funds developing products that people will not buy. History attests to many products that were commercial failures in spite of being technological breakthroughs.

A formal approach to this customer-focused marketing is known as SIVA (Solution, Information, Value, Access). This system is basically the 4Ps renamed and reworded to provide a customer focus.

The SIVA Model provides a demand/customer centric version alternative to the well-known 4Ps supply side model (product, price, place, promotion) of marketing management.

Product → Solution
Promotion → Information
Price → Value
Place → Access

The four elements of the SIVA model are:

1. *Solution*: How appropriate is the solution to the customers problem/need?
2. *Information*: Does the customer know about the solution, and if so how, who from, do they know enough to let them make a buying decision?
3. *Value:* Does the customer know the value of the transaction, what it will cost, what are the benefits, what might they have to sacrifice, what will be their reward?
4. *Access*: Where can the customer find the solution? How easily/locally/remotely can they buy it and take delivery?

This model was proposed by Chekitan Dev and Don Schultz in the Marketing Management Journal of the American Marketing Association, and presented by them in Market Leader—the journal of the Marketing Society in the UK.

The model focuses heavily on the customer and how they view the transaction.

Product Focus

In a product innovation approach, the company pursues product innovation, then tries to develop a market for the product. Product innovation drives the process and marketing research is conducted primarily to ensure that a profitable market segment(s) exists for the innovation. The rationale is that customers may not know what options will be available to them in the future so we should not expect them to tell us what they will buy in the future. However, marketers can aggressively over-pursue product innovation and try to overcapitalize on a niche. When pursuing a product innovation approach, marketers must ensure that they have a varied and multi-tiered approach to product innovation. It is claimed that if Thomas Edison depended on marketing research he would have produced larger candles rather than inventing light bulbs. Many firms, such as research and development focused companies, successfully focus on product innovation (Such as Nintendo who constantly change the way Video games are played). Many purists doubt whether this is really a form of marketing orientation at all, because of the ex post status of consumer research. Some even question whether it is marketing.

- An emerging area of study and practice concerns internal marketing, or how employees are trained and managed to deliver the brand in a way that positively impacts the acquisition and retention of customers (employer branding).
- Diffusion of innovations research explores how and why people adopt new products, services and ideas.
- A relatively new form of marketing uses the Internet and is called *internet marketing* or more generally e-marketing, affiliate marketing, desktop advertising or online marketing. It typically tries to perfect the segmentation strategy used in traditional marketing. It targets its audience more precisely, and is sometimes called personalized marketing or *one-to-one marketing*.
- With consumers' eroding attention span and willingness to give time to advertising messages, marketers are turning to forms of permission marketing such as branded content, custom media and reality marketing.
- The use of herd behaviour in marketing.

In an article entitled "Swarming the shelves: How shops can exploit people's herd mentality to increase sales", *The Economist* recently reported a recent conference in Rome on the subject of the simulation of adaptive human behaviour. Mechanisms to increase impulse buying and get people "to buy more by playing on the herd instinct" were shared. The basic idea is that people will buy more of products that are seen to be popular, and several feedback mechanisms to get product popularity information to consumers are mentioned, including smart-cart technology and the use of Radio Frequency Identification Tag technology. A "swarm-moves" model was introduced by a Princeton researcher, which is appealing to supermarkets because it can "increase sales without the need to give people discounts." Large retailers Wal-Mart in the United States and Tesco in Britain plan to test the technology in spring 2007.

Other recent studies on the "power of social influence" include an "artificial music market in which some 14,000 people downloaded previously unknown songs" (Columbia University, New York); a Japanese chain of convenience stores which orders its products based on "sales data from department stores and research companies;" a Massachusetts company exploiting knowledge of social networking to improve sales; and online retailers who are increasingly informing consumers about "which products are popular with like-minded consumers" (*e.g.*, Amazon, eBay).

Criticism of Marketing

Some aspects of marketing, especially promotion, are the subject of criticism. It is especially problematic in classical economic theory, which is based on the assumption that supply and demand are independent. However, product promotion is an attempt coming from the supply side to influence demand. In this way producer market power is attained as measured by profits that would not be realized under a free market. Then the argument follows that non-free markets are imperfect and lead to production and consumption of suboptimal amounts of the product.

Critics acknowledge that marketing has legitimate uses in connecting goods and services to the consumers who want them. Critics also point out that marketing techniques have been used to achieve morally dubious ends by businesses, governments and criminals. Critics see a systemic social evil inherent in marketing (see *No Logo*, Bill Hicks, Marxism or Commercial Alert). Marketing is accused of creating ruthless exploitation of both consumers and workers by treating people as commodities whose purpose is to consume (see Fashion victim).

Most marketers believe that marketing techniques themselves are amoral. While it is ethically neutral, it can be used for negative purposes, such as selling unhealthy food to obese people or selling SUVs in a time of global warming, but it can also have a positive influence on consumer welfare.

The Observer's survey among 1,206 UK adult consumers in 2001 highlighted some of the stark changes our society has gone through in the last two decades. This raises a question on the effectiveness of the CIM's definition of marketing (anticipating, identifying and satisfying customer needs profitably), mainly in consumer marketing. There are similar concerns in industrial markets, also known as business-to-business or B2B. Industrial market segmentation attempts to provide some answers.

Core marketing elements such as segmentation, targeting and positioning are still relevant in the modern (or post-modern) world. However, they are complex topics that need a high level of effort, intelligent thinking as well as resources to be implemented successfully. A definitive statement cannot be made whether the conventional marketing concept is applicable in today's environment. Its relevance is very much situational and depends on many factors such as the product, the segment, time, location, political and economic conditions and the inner workings of a company.

However, some scholars such as Stephen Brown challenge the marketing concept in an extreme language. Their statements, sometimes unfair, are relevant, which is why Post-Modern Marketing 2 was chosen as a key reference point for this chapter.

On the one hand, Brown makes positive statements about marketing, *e.g.* "marketing is endowed with considerable personal charm and has enjoyed more than its fair share of conquests" (Brown, 1998 : 16); and "indeed, the increasing academic attention that is being devoted to marketing and consumption-related phenomena by non-business disciplines such as sociology, anthropology and history; far from being the second-hand rose of the scholarship, marketing is now something of a fashion leader" (p. 17).

On the other hand, he condemns marketing by saying "marketing has to decide whether to expose its intellectual nakedness or press itself against the searing heat of post-modernism" (p. 17); and using phrases such as "mid-life crisis" (p. 23); "in decline; failing; anachronistic; being abandoned; no longer appropriate; in an unprecedented state of crisis; delivered nothing of value; failure; confusion; misunderstanding; occasional inexplicable hitting of the jackpot" (p. 21).

This apparent love-hate relationship is proof in itself that even a skeptics find it difficult to deny the contribution that marketing has made and can make to customer satisfaction and economic value. It has contributed to both customers' and suppliers' quality of life by selecting profitable customer satisfaction as its sole objective. The marketing concept, together with other business disciplines, helped the UK to make the transition from a 19th-century manufacturing economy to a modern model of success in the service industry, creating an economic growth period never seen before in the United Kingdom.

Marketing has helped create value through customized products, no-questions-asked refund policies, comfortable cars, environmental attention, shopkeepers' smile, and guaranteed delivery dates. Even some government departments address the public not as 'the Queen's subjects' or 'the applicants' any more but as 'customers.' Of course all of the above is done for economic or political gain, for better or worse. Despite all this achievement, to dismiss marketing as a failure is unfair.

Marketing also helps companies avoid unnecessary R&D, operational and sales costs by helping to develop products because customers want them, not for the sake of innovation. Another success is the now commonly implemented value—pricing principle, whereby a product or service is sold for the price the customer is willing to pay, not on a cost-plus basis. This way, both suppliers and customers get a fair deal.

In the context of segmentation, Brown suggests that "the traditional, linear, step-by-step marketing model of analysis, planning, implementation and control no longer seems applicable, appropriate or even pertinent to what is actually happening on the ground" (pp. 23-24). If Mr. Brown had studied "the ground" before making his statement, he would have realised that companies are successful the world over precisely because they implement this model.

They segment their markets, relate their products and services to them, define their value proposition and serve their customers accordingly. Examples are General Electric, HSBC, PriceWaterhouseCoopers, Smiths Aerospace, BAE Systems, BOC Edwards, Weir Group and the BT Group to name but a few. A brief visit to their websites can make this point clear.

Stephen Brown also has a constructive suggestion: "I reckon we need more passion in marketing, not less; it is time we banished banishing passion from works of marketing scholarship" (p. 256). This refers mainly to promotion, which is only one element within the marketing concept. The truth is that marketing today leads the way in segmentation, innovation, pricing, product management, distribution, and last but not least, promotion.

After all the contribution as well as further potential, to deny its successes and try to reduce it to only promotion is a great injustice to the marketing profession as well as to academic insight. Contrary to Brown's suggestion in his final paragraph (p. 257), we need objectivity, rigour, quantification, models, relationships, paradigm shifts and (some application of) science.

Construction Marketing

Due to increased competition, privatization and globalization, marketing and business development have become increasingly important functions in all construction organizations. Marketing research, corporate branding and public relations are increasingly being seen as vital in a marketplace typified by sophisticated and demanding clients and customers, and a socially and environmentally aware general public and media.

SALES

Sales are the activities involved in selling products or services in return for money or other compensation. It is an act of completion of a commercial activity.

The "deal is closed", means the customer has consented to the proposed product or service by making full or partial payment (as in case of installments) to the seller.

Academically, selling is thought of as a part of marketing, however, the two disciplines are completely different. Sales often forms a separate grouping in a corporate structure, employing separate specialist operatives known as *salesmen* (singular: *salesman*). Sales is considered by many to be a sort of persuading "art". Contrary to popular belief, the methodological approach of selling refers to a *systematic process of repetitive and measurable milestones, by which a salesman relates his offering of a product or service in return enabling the buyer to achieve his goal in an economic way.*

Agents

Agents in the sales process can be defined as representing either side of the sales process for example:

- *Sales broker or seller agency or seller agent*: This is a traditional sales person role where the sales person represents a person or company on the selling end of the deal.
- *Buyers broker or buyer brokerage*: This is where the sales person represents the consumer making the purchase. This is most often applied in large transactions.
- *Disclosed dual agent*: This is where the sales person represents both parties in the sale and acts as a mediator for the transaction. The role of the sales person here is to over see that both parties receive an honest and fair deal, and is responsible to both.
- *Transaction broker*: This is where the sales person doesn't represent either party, but handles the transaction only. This is where the seller owes no responsibility to either party getting a fair or honest deal, just that all of the papers are handled properly.
- *Sales outsourcing*: This is direct branded representation where the sales reps are recruited, hired, and managed by an external entity but hold quotas, represent themselves as the brand of the client, and report all activities (through their own sales management channels) back to the client. It is akin to a virtual extension of a sales force (see *Sales Outsourcing* entry).
- *Sales managers*: It is the goal of a qualified and talented sales manager to implement various sales strategies and management techniques in order to facilitate improved profits and increased sales volume. They are also responsible for coordinating the sales and marketing department as well as oversight concerning the fair and honest execution of the sales process by his agents.
- *Salespersons*: The primary function of professional sales is to generate and close leads, educate prospects, fill

needs and satisfy wants of consumers appropriately, and therefore turn prospective customers into actual ones. The successful questioning to understand a customer's goal, the further creation of a valuable solution by communicating the necessary information that encourages a buyer to achieve his goal at an economic cost is the responsibility of the sales person or the sales engine (*e.g.* Internet, vending machine etc).

Sales Techniques

The sale can be made through:

- Direct sales, involving person to person contact—
  - Buying Facilitation Method.
- Pro forma sales.
- Agency-based—
  - Sales agents (real estate, manufacturing).
  - Sales Outsourcing through direct branded representation (see Sales Outsourcing entry).
  - Transaction sales.
  - Consultative sales.
  - Complex sales.
  - Consignment.
  - Tele-marketing or tele-sales.
  - Retail or consumer.
- Door-to-Door or travelling salesman.
- Request for proposal is an invitation for suppliers, through a bidding process, to submit a proposal on a specific product or service. An RFP is usually part of a complex sales process, also known as enterprise sales.
- Business-to-business—Business-to-business sales are much more relationship based owing to the lack of emotional attachment to the products in question. Industrial/ Professional Sales is selling from one business to another.
- *Electronic*—
  - Web—Business-to-business and business-to-consumer.

    - Electronic Data Interchange (EDI) is a set of standards for structuring information to be electronically exchanged between and within businesses.
- Indirect, human-mediated but with indirect contact—
    - Mail-order.

Sales and Marketing Relationship

Marketing plays a very important part in sales. If the marketing department generates a potential customers list, it can be beneficial for sales. The marketing department's goal is to bring people to the sales team using promotional techniques such as advertising, sales promotion, publicity and public relations. In most large corporations, the marketing department is structured in a similar fashion to the sales department and the managers of these teams must coordinate efforts in order to drive profits and business success. Driving more customers "through the door" gives the sales department a better chance by ratio of selling their product to the consumer. There may also be a downside to this phenomenon. Very often (for legal reasons, *e.g.*, in non-store retailing) companies have to provide credit to customers. This may cause a conflict between the sales department on the one hand and the credit department on the other hand. See Burez & Van den Poel (2007) for potential solutions to this problem.

Single Purchases

Organizations seldom profit from single purchases made by first-time customers. Normally they rely on repeat business to generate the profit that they need. However, there are some industries which have a business model based on one time only sales relationship. These tend to be the sale of very expensive, unusual household products such as houses and new and used cars. The economic reason for this behaviour is that these items are usually unique. Consumers buy people not products. Consumers will often pay more and accept less quality if they like and trust the sales person.

Criticisms

In capitalist apologetics, the purpose of selling is to help a customer realize his or her goals in an economic fashion. This assumption neglects the fact that buyer and seller may not have the same interests. Even if the selling organization recognizes that its sustainability depends on the maintenance of a healthy relationship with repeat customers, the salesperson does not necessarily share that goal.

Many sales professionals are characterized by their short-term goals, a desire for quick returns on effort, and not the long-term building of relationships that the most successful sales people undertake. This dysfunctional behaviour is encouraged by:

- Incentives of salespeople to increase their total number of sales, especially where retailers keep track of sales or offer commission-based salaries.
- Incentives from the manufactures of products or the companies of service providers to salespeople to sell their products where other similar products offered by competitors are offered.
- The incentive to sell a customer a product that is in need of being cleared out, despite the fact that a customer may be better to wait for the new product.
- The pressure exerted by sales managers on sales executives to perform month on month. Sales executives to relieve themselves of pressure, engage in deceitful practices.

Salespersons recognize that customers having been deceived are unlikely to buy a similar product for a long time. Coincidently, the salesperson has no incentive to offer any extra quality of service to encourage a long-term relationship. This behaviour is generally true only of business-to-consumer sales.

I. The Hotel Marketing Association HMA: Case Studies

The HMA is the official branch of the Chartered Institute of Marketing specifically for the hotel industry. The HMA is supported by many of the hotel companies in the UK and its membership comprises, sales, marketing and operations personnel from small and large hotels and companies alike. The one thing our members all have in common is a desire to learn more about hotel marketing. We exist to provide education in hotel marketing, to raise the standard of hotel marketing and to endorse good marketing practice. We also provide an opportunity for members to network with others from the industry and share ideas and opinions.

II. Hospitality Sales and Marketing Association International (HSMAI)

Mission Statement: To be the leading source for sales and marketing information, knowledge, business development, and networking for professionals in tourism, travel and hospitality.

HSMAI is a global organization of sales and marketing professionals representing all segments of the hospitality industry. With a strong focus on education, HSMAI has become the industry champion in identifying and communicating trends in the hospitality industry while operating as a leading voice for both hospitality and sales and marketing management disciplines, as well as connecting its members with customers. Founded in 1927, HSMAI is an individual membership organization comprised of nearly 7,000 members from 35 countries and chapters worldwide. HSMAI's Americas Region, headquartered in McLean, VA, consists of 38 chapters in three countries. HSMAI's European Region, headquartered in Oslo, Norway, consists of five national chapters in Europe. The Asia Pacific Region is under development. The HSMAI Foundation was established in 1983 to serve as the research and educational arm of HSMAI.

The HSMAI Foundation

The HSMAI Foundation was established in 1983 to serve as the research and educational arm of the Hospitality Sales and Marketing Association International, and is now part of the HSMAI Global organization. Its mission has evolved to improving the body of knowledge available to hospitality sales and marketing executives through information.

The HSMAI foundation's research publications include the new "Travel Marketer's Guide to Social Media and Social Networks," produced in partnership with the Travel Industry.

In addition, the foundation provides scholarships to students in university-based hospitality programmes whose focus of study is sales and marketing. eConnect, a one-stop portal to global information and resources on hospitality sales and marketing topics, is a service provided by the HSMAI foundation through its Research Partnership programme, to create a repository for information on and research into today's most important industry issues.

III. Hotel Online Special Report

Hotel Common Sense. "A Bakers Dozen" of Strategies for Hotel Sales and Marketing Professionals. A Bakers Dozen equals 13. It means 12 loaves plus (+) one extra for luck.

While business is brisk today in many parts of the industry, planning makes "luck" much more achievable.

1. *Learn everything about the services and product you will be promoting:* This first step is perhaps the most obvious requirement for any successful sales professional, yet one that is often overlooked especially by those individuals who may have additional responsibilities at their hotel. Many smaller properties hold their general manager responsible for the sales and marketing efforts and while this can work, knowledge of the entire hotel is essential.

   Particulars include:

   - Personally inspecting every type of accommodation in your hotel. Learn the differences and potential benefits of each type and how they can be of value to different customers. This tour should not be a one time event—quarterly tours will keep you aware of changes in the hotel and can also help management to be better aware of potential problems.

- Maintain your awareness of the property of the whole, This includes parking areas, access points to the hotel and the all important curb appeal.
- If you have work with an adjacent restaurant or other external service that is part of your offerings, regularly assess their quality and how it affects your guests' satisfaction.
- Regularly visit the front of the house AND the "heart of the hotel" *Everyday*. This should be routine for managers, but for the staff to see that the sales professionals are aware of their contributions can mean a great deal in staff morale.

2. *Learn everything about the services and product of those hotels that you will be competing with:* Effective sales professionals know who is in their competitive set, and everything about them. They learn the strengths and weaknesses of their competitors and plan accordingly as they try to increase market share at the expense of their competitors.
3. *Listen Better:* Do not prepare your response before the other person has actually delivered their message. While it is critical to be able to handle objections, respond to what your client actually is interested in or says.
4. *Regularly communicate with the entire hotel staff on sales and marketing programmes, challenges and needs—remember, the results of sales and marketing efforts affect everyone on staff regardless of title or position:* If you are the general manager, you already have regular communications on operations, but not necessarily on sales and marketing activities. If you are primarily in sales and marketing, look for ways to positively inform hotel staff about what is important and going on both today and long-term. The most successful hotels are those that have open dialogue and build pride by inclusion of all staff.
5. *Constantly assess time management:* The 80-20 rule of priorities and value remains true much of the time. 80 per cent of our profits often come from 20 per cent of the client base. The same hold true for problem areas. The

question needs to be not are we doing things "right", but are we doing the "right" things correctly? Are we trying to provide services for the "right customers" for our hotel? If our hotel was designed for youth groups, then targeting business executives is not likely to be successful.

6. *Set realistic occupancy targets that become the foundation of the hotel's operating budgets:* Budgets are often finally approved by the ownership or management company in a remote location, but the first step of any budget is to understand probable demand. This means accurate records must be maintained and trends identified. Be able to justify why RevPAR, occupancy or revenue targets should be at a certain level based on facts, market conditions and the positioning of your property.

   Budgets are often controversial and at times seem unachievable. The best time to project accurately for the next year is right after that period has finished for this year. For example, if one waits until September to project occupancy for the following January to December, there can significant changes in market conditions, staffing or simply a memory lapse that can seriously undermine accuracy. If one makes a draft of the budget for following April in May after the income statement and market analysis have been reviewed, the chances are that the projections will be able to be justified and more accurate than trying to prepare 12 months in one action. As a general manager or sales professional, you know the cost of turnover from people realizing they cannot achieve unattainable budgets.

7. *Plan, coordinate and implement a hotel specific marketing budgets annually*: As the marketing and operations team must work together, we must recognize the need to "plan the work and work the plan." There needs to be an annual plan that is worked and measured at least monthly. While no plan is perfect, researching trends, evaluating the hotels positioning through a SWOT analysis and identifying the likely customer base is the basis of every plan. Even if your hotel is primarily walk-

in business or one night stays, understanding their referral points, price breaks and booking trends is essential to lasting success.

8. *Everybody sells*: Effective sales and marketing professionals adopted this mantra years ago. Every member of your staff belongs to a family or a church or a social organization or some other group that occasionally has the need for your hotel's services. Sometimes incentives are the key to get staff to think about recommending your hotel and other times it is simply asking them to help themselves by offering the information about your hotel.
9. *Training must be maintained and increased for sales and marketing professionals*: In good times of a sellers' market, many hotels unfortunately tend to act as order takers because the belief is that there will always be another customer. In hard times or a buyer's market, the skills of effective sales professionals become obvious. What we as an industry need to realize is that there are always business cycles and those trends are not always self-evident. Most hotel brands also have excellent training programmes available, as well as services provided by state and provincial hospitality associations.

   Additional training is available in a variety of formats from a range of excellent sources such as:

   - Hospitality Sales and Marketing Association International (HSMAI) www.hsmai.org.
   - American Society of Association Executives—www.asaecenter.org/.
   - American Hotel & Lodging Association www.ahla.com.
   - Educational Institute of AH&LA www.ei-ahla.org.
   - Meeting Professionals International—www.mpiweb.org.
   - Professional Convention Management Association www.pcma.org.

- ❖ Society of Corporate Meeting Planners—www.scmp.org.
- ❖ Society of Government Meeting Planners www.sgmp.org.
- ❖ Asian American Hotel Owners Association www.aahoa.com.

10. *Pay attention to the "human" resource role with increasing intensity in those who will be acting as sales and marketing professionals*: Recruit and select people wisely. Pay competitively or better and lead in incentives. Recognize your team regularly with "thank you's "and expressions of appreciation. Retain the champions by whatever it takes to keep them. Choose people who are self-driven team players and who are not afraid to hear "no".
11. *Review your market analysis monthly and evaluate its effectiveness on the hotel income statement*: As in #5 of time management and #6 of realistic forecasts, successful hotels know which kind of customer base is profitable for their hotel. Effective sales professionals and general managers help themselves and their hotel's owner by understanding how to assess which customers best fit their hotel's offerings. Markets can shift and what used to be a tour market might shift to a youth or other SMERF demand generator. Watching your trends if essential.
12. *Know your customers—"Up close and personal"*: The legendary sales and marketing professionals are those who know the base of their clients and interact with them regularly. Industry icons ranging from Conrad Hilton to Horst Schulze to Ian Schrager to Mike Leven would tell you a major part of their companies' success is attributable to knowing major customers, regardless of title.

- ❖ Do you as a general manager know the top five customers of your hotel?
- ❖ Do you as sales and marketing professional personally know the top ten customers of your hotel?

- ❖ Do you visit or contact the top 20 accounts at least once a month?
- ❖ Do you know each month if these top 20 accounts' volume has changed and why?
- ❖ Do you visit or contact the top 50 accounts at least twice a year?

13. *Maintain rate parity through ongoing revenue management*: Use whatever systems you need to track demand, denials, booking pace, rate break points and other revenue management strategies. Be certain to use the information on your hotel's particular competitive set via the Smith Travel reports or other completive data available to you regularly. Technology today coupled with someone who will take the time to evaluate data makes a tremendous difference.

IV. Hotel Marketing Resources, Inc.

At hotel marketing resources, inc. we understand what hotels need for success in today's climate of uncertainty and ultra-tight resources. We focus on result-centered solutions tailored to fit your market and your property requirements. We focus on cost-effective hotel sales and marketing initiatives meant to ensure that you get the most from your hotel marketing dollars.

A sample of how we provide sales and marketing solutions for the hospitality industry:

- ❖ Hotel marketing direction, hotel sales consulting and hotel sales training.
- ❖ Consulting for sales management of multi-unit and multi-franchise companies.
- ❖ Develop quick-action hotel sales and marketing plans designed just for your market and your property requirements.
- ❖ Plan and direct a critical path for sales and marketing efforts for hotels in transition.
- ❖ Provide hotel sales training for all experience levels.
- ❖ Sales training with a focus on developing new market segments for your hotel such as government and the travel industry.

- Personalized consulting to evaluate the efficiency of your sales process and provide recommendations for improvement.
- More services are available—just ask us!

Let HMR help you put the pieces together for sales and marketing plans, sales office automation, hotel internet marketing and opening new sources of business. We know how hotel sales and marketing work together to get results in today's highly competitive and volatile environment.

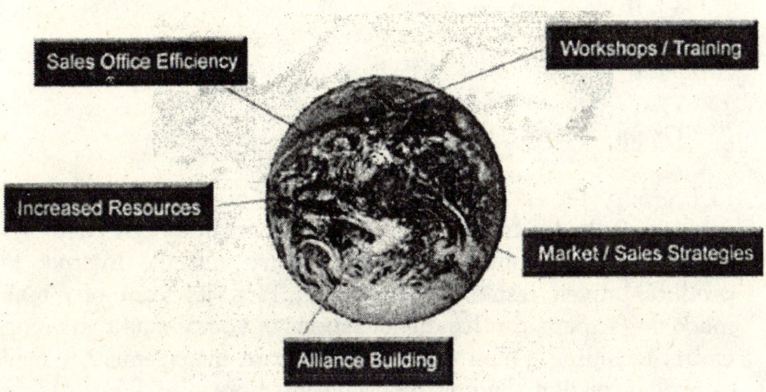

HMR Services

Customized sales and training solutions for the hotel industry

Let HMR Be Your

"Special Forces" In Sales and Marketing

- Extend your marketing department and resources.
- Pre-opening sales and marketing.
- Sales lead generation and tele-marketing.
- Hiring strategies/interviewing and selection.
- Public relations/community outreach.
- Special events planning.

Efficiency is the Key to

A Successful Sales Office

- Improve sales office efficiency.
- Developing integrated sales systems and procedures.
- Team building.
- Time management for effective sales.
- Incentive programmes.
- Sales department audits.
- Sales skill training.

Alliances

LET Group

LET group, inc. is the leading provider of Internet marketing solutions to the top travel and hospitality companies. LET combines its knowledge of the hospitality industry and the Internet to produce proven results for its clients. Plus, its team of e-mail marketing experts can handle all aspects of your e-mail marketing efforts including e-mail collection, database management, e-mail campaign creation, sending, reporting and more.

Unirez by Pegasus

Unirez, is a leading provider of reservations services and integrated technology solutions to the hospitality industry. They provide distribution channels for seamless GDS distribution in Saber, Galileo, World span and Amadeus, plus Internet connectivity to key sites such as Travel Web, Travelocity, Expedia, Orbitz, Hotwire and hundreds more.

Hotel Sales and Catering Pro

PMS is known for Sales Pro or Sales and Catering Pro; hotel sales software designed for either full service or limited service hotels. Hotel professionals with more than 100 years of lodging industry experience design both software programmes. The products are priced at a fraction of the cost of comparable programmes and are easy to use. Both programmes come with a 100 per cent Satisfaction Guarantee.

Innovata/FTD

Innovata provides content and distribution solutions to the hotel industry. It aggregates and distributes travel data including airline, hotel and rental cars travel data plus passenger train and destination information. Innovata also owns the Federal Travel Directory, which is accessed directly from the GSA website. This directory is used by hundreds of thousands of federal travellers every month. An enhanced listing with the FTD can help a hotel effectively reach the government traveller.

Point B Communications

Point B is an advertising agency that for a quarter of a century has been helping hospitality clients expand markets and increase revenues. It specializes in the hotel industry and provides both property level (field experiences) and national brand marketing experience. Point B repeatedly earns the prestigious HSMAI Adrian and Golden Bell awards; in 2002 this innovative agency won 11 HSMAI awards.

North Star Travel Media/HTI

Over 85 per cent of travel agents and corporate travel planners rank Hotel and Travel Index as the hotel information resource they use most often. HTI reaches travel professionals through the traditional directory and the new www.htihotelink.com, automated directory. Both are powerful tools for target marketing to travel agents, corporate travel planners, or meeting planners.

Tony Soluri Photography

Tony Soluri is a Chicago based photographer who specializes in architectural and interior photography that incorporates "lifestyle" with them. Soluri works with advertising and editorial clients. A contributing photographer to Architectural Digest magazine for 15 years, hotel and resort photography comprise a large part of his work. He has photographed over 100 hotels and resorts including The Fairmont Chicago, The Broadmoor, The Grand Wailea Resort and Spa Maui, various Embassy Suites, Marriotts, Sheratons and over 60 Hyatt Hotels.

Pre-Paid Legal Services, Inc.

A pioneer of prepaid legal services, Pre-Paid Legal Services, Inc. has set the bar for individual and employment prepaid legal plans. With over 30 years of experience Pre-Paid offers a wide variety of benefits ranging from contract & document reviews, wills and trust preparation, motor vehicle services, trial defense services, IRS audit legal services, identity theft protection, and much more.

Driving Your Revenue

- What can hotel marketing resources do for you?
- Total sales training.
- Workshops.
- Revenue Drivers.
- Market specific direct sales.
- Strategic sales planning/action plan.
- Integrated advertising campaigns.
- Understanding and developing new market segments.
- Multi-unit sales management.
- Sales office automation.
- Motivating sales bonus systems.
- Tailored solutions to property specific marketing challenges.
- Conflict resolution.
- Market analysis.
- Competitive analysis.

Workshops/Training

Hotel Sales Training

- Sales team training—Sales office audit.
- Sales team training—Sales and marketing training.
- Sales Team Training—ROI—Focusing on demand generators.
- Sales team training—electronic Distribution.
- Sales Team Training—The government market.
- Sales management training.
- Sales team training—building a sales team.
- Team training—selling strategy.

Sales Office Audit

This hotel sales audit is a structured in-depth evaluation of every major area of your sales operation. It verifies which sales office functions are working at maximum efficiency. It also prioritizes the areas for improvement with potentially the most pay-off in effectiveness and profitability. *Hotel Marketing Resources* will carefully review every aspect of the sales function; provide you with a post-evaluation review, and an action plan for improvement.

Part One

Evaluate the efficiency of the sales system:

- Master file system.
- Function book.
- Group room control log.
- Contract audit and synchronization to GRC and function book.
- Effectiveness of current sales reports.
- Electronic distribution channels: brand website, GDS, property specific site.
- Trace system standards.

- Sales office materials and collateral.
- Review and use of business information reports such as the STAR report.
- Current sales action plan.

Part Two

Evaluate and understand the effectiveness of you sales team:

- Evaluate sales activity goals.
- Weekly activity goals.
- Scheduled meetings.
- Staffing levels.
- Future training to continue to develop your sales power.
- Bonus and reward programme.

Part Three

Evaluate the revenue performance of your sales team:

- Current year's budgeted occupancy, ADR, REVPAR, total revenue goals.
- Past year's performance and market conditions.
- Year to date performance.
- Current rate strategy.
- Comparison of rates and performance to competitive set.

ASAP Marketing Workshop

Hotel Sales Workshops

Today's hotel marketing environment is rough—volatile, unpredictable, requiring hotels to step up their sales and marketing efforts, despite the constrain of ever-tightening budgets. To do this successfully takes a different mind-set, one designed for this environment—and ASAP marketing has it.

The purpose of the ASAP Marketing Hotel Sales Workshop is fourfold:

1. To enable you tc sell and market more.
2. To help you put into play assets that do not draw down on already tight budgets.
3. To show you how to win the trust and confidence of customers and other allies.
4. To help you dominate your home turf while sealing out competitors.

- Part one of the workshop: What goes into this mind-set shift?
- Part two of the workshop: Getting inside the ASAP four-step programme.
- Always plan but keep it simple. What's in it and why?
- Secure your customers, allies and partners. How to do it?
- Arm with the right tools. What should be YOUR weapons of choice?
- Put "freebies" to work for you. They're there. Want some?

Getting Others to Sell for You

A Hotel Marketing Resource, Inc. Online Workshop

This is a workshop that targets the top demand generators in your hotel's marketing area to ensure they are the centerpiece of your selling plan. HMR provides dozens of "tried and true" sales tips to help you build your business. Our objective is to help you to see all of the opportunity that is in your backyard and assist you in building a plan to use your resources to capture that business.

During the workshops each attendee will complete an outline which can become the basis for your ongoing selling strategy. The action required by the hotel will be discussed and can easily be translated into your monthly selling plan for next year.

The Demand Generators Workshop is excellent for people new to hotel sales or a great refresher for experienced sales people who are looking for new ideas. This workshop is especially exciting in a group that has various levels of experience because we set the stage for a great idea exchange.

Our sessions will literally go from A-Z and cover everything from airport business to travel agency business. Each module will be approximately one hour and are typically scheduled one week apart.

Your Training Investment

- *Payment options:* HMR, Inc. accepts online payments of Visa, American Express, MasterCard and Discover or advance payment by personal or company check.
- *Cancellation and refund policy:* Full refund (minus $25 processing fee) for written cancellations received at least seventy-two hours before the scheduled day for the workshop. Cancellations after seventy-two hours may be rescheduled for another workshop to take place within the next 30 days.
- *Maximum online seminar attendees:* To provide you with the best training experience HMR has a maximum of 10 attendees per training session.

HMR, Inc. accepts online payment with these major credit cards—MasterCard, VISA, American Express, and DuCover.

Getting What's Yours to Take

Sales Team Training—Electronic Distribution

This is a workshop that teaches you how to get the most productive return from your e-commerce. We will focus, first, on the importance of always maintaining complete and timely information in your own GDS database. Then we will get into the heart of effective Internet marketing. You'll complete an action plan for your hotel and receive valuable sales tips.

1. *Outside of the Internet channels*: The importance of your GDS. For most hotels GDS is still giving your biggest

room numbers. It all starts with and comes back to your GDS information. In most hotels it is still your main distribution channel. To make it work for you, you need to keep your GDS straight at all times.

- What your system and database should have in it.
- Your last audit and what should you check.
- Analyzing denials and regrets—the secret weapon.
- Updating schedule—what's acceptable.
- Current data and inventory.
- Fallback rates, rate tiers, and SRP.
- Brand support.

2. Build the Right Foundation:

    - *The Centerpiece*: Direct- to-Customer.
    - *Search Engine Savvy*—Can you be found?

3. *The Internet*—are you using the Internet as a distribution channel? We will do an overview of Internet marketing and discuss some effective strategies to better understand this powerful revenue opportunity.

    - Corporate brand website.
    - Travel websites.
    - Independent hotel website.

4. Direction online distribution

    - Hotel website,
    - Brand website, and
    - Destination websites.

5. Indirect online distribution

    - *Agency*—example: Orbitz.com,
    - Opaque rate models—example: Priceline.com,

- ❖ Merchant models—example: Hotels.com,

6. *Trends*: What's happening today and what will tomorrow be on the Internet,
7. E-Commerce action plan, and
8. Tips.

When you finish this workshop you should be able to

- ❖ develop a functional action plan for electronic distribution.
- ❖ understand the various distribution opportunities.
- ❖ identify e-commerce business opportunities.

Length of Workshop

Webinar—Three one hour sessions.

Is the Government Giving you the Business?

Sales Team Training—The Government Market
GuvBiz—Is the Government Giving you the Business.

A Hotel Marketing Resource, Inc. Online Workshop

The federal government, civilian and military, is the single biggest user of hotel rooms in the country. This workshop is a "tool kit" for penetrating, marketing and selling to this lucrative market. We begin with the basics about the scope, size and unique characteristics of this market. We then examine this business as a good fit for our hotel and just how much government business might be right for you. Next we develop the elements of an action strategy to work this particular market in your area. We start with what you currently know about your government business and, as the planning session progresses; we add dozens of practical tips to jump-start or to augment your action plan. In addition, to help you get access to and to ask the right questions of your government prospects, we introduce some of the key "code" words and regulations that define this market. You will also learn about great Internet sites, some that provide on-line access to a wealth of useful information and others that permit on-line registration for essential government ID numbers.

Getting to know the language, at least some key "code" words will help give you access. Plus, understanding a few regulations will help you to ask the right questions of your prospects. How much government business is right for you? That's a question that we will help you to answer during this workshop. After you've determined if this business is right for your hotel you'll need a working strategy to for better targeting the government market. We'll start with what you know currently about your government business and add ideas and actions as we go through the workshop. This gets to the heart of it—you'll receive dozens of ideas for what to do and actions to take to jumpstart your action plan. Using the power of the Internet makes it easy to tackle this huge segment. You will be introduced to sites that are a wealth of information and also allow on-line registration for important government ID numbers.

Outline

- Getting into the basics—facts to know and gov. speak 101 and 201.
- Is the government market right for you?
- Building your government marketing programme.
- Marketing ideas and general information for the civilian government segment.
- Marketing ideas and general information for the military segment.
- Internet resources.

Who should Take this Class?

- Whether you're new to the government market or experienced but seriously looking for new ideas this workshop is designed to get you there—fast.

When you finish you should be able to

- understand some key words and regulations needed to do business with this segment.
- decide if federal government business is right for your hotel.
- develop a basic written selling strategy for this segment.
- incorporate workshop marketing tips into our selling plan.
- access key Internet sites to learn even more about the government market.

Length of Workshop

- Webinar—3 sessions of 1 hour each.
- Live-one site—One half day.
- For more details and pricing of this workshop and others please feel free to contact us.
- HMR, inc. accepts online payment with these major credit cards.

HOSPITALITY CONSULTING AND TRAINING

Consultations

Independent Property Consulting and Coaching Package

The world of hotel sales and revenue management is changing at warp speed! Just because a property is an independent hotel doesn't mean that you have to be shut out of expert advice that can strain your budget. We at CVCT understand your concerns and have developed this package especially for you!

As an independent property, we understand that you may not have the resources available to your franchise competitors but you also need support in being fast and efficient and this is what we are all about! This package is a three month experience that ramps up your sales and revenue management team with tools they can use immediately—remember, *it's not the big that eat the small; it's the fast that eat the slow!*

The package includes:

- ❖ A property visit to get to know your market and your sales force.
- ❖ Analysis of sales, revenue management and yield processes with recommendations.
- ❖ A complete report including recommendations on how to make their processes faster and more efficient.
- ❖ A sales and revenue management plan and budget.
- ❖ A front desk sales training seminar or a customer service programme for your associates.
- ❖ A structured weekly coaching experience for two months with a full recap report to key contacts each week.

The property will have a dedicated person to work with who will also share best practices that have been successfully implemented at hotels like yours. All of this at a price that you can afford—a small investment in the team to maximize revenue in 2008 and beyond!

Email us carol@carolverret.com or call (303) 618-4065 to find out when you can get started boosting your revenue and REVPAR!

*Property visit expenses such as air, ground transportation, accommodation and meals are not included in the package price.

Marketing and Sales Diagnostic

This consultation is ideal for those properties under-performing in their respective markets. It can be implemented for a single property or groups of hotels and is a detailed examination of the following:

- ❖ Effective use of franchise and industry resources.
- ❖ Sales department audit including the organization and effectiveness of the sales office procedures and personnel.

- The General Manager's role in supporting the sales operation and promoting the hotel in the community.
- Reservations and front desk sales skills.
- Analysis of and assistance in the development of an effective Marketing Plan.
- Recommendations and action plans based on the findings above.

This analysis can be expanded to provide training and ongoing support at the client's discretion.

Transforming the Sales Organization

This consultation is designed for sales offices and organizations that find that their processes and procedures are not aligned with the technological changes in the way that sales is conducted today. We interview the key members of the department to identify their concerns in a supportive manner and enlist them in the process. It includes an analysis of the following and a blueprint for transforming the sales organization as well as ongoing support until the identified and agreed upon change is established. We also identify areas of skill set development required to support the staff in successfully implementing change.

- Organization of the department and its effectiveness.
- Analysis of the processes and procedures of the organization.
- The internal communications flow.
- Activity tracking and client communications integration.
- Revenue generation versus revenue potential.
- Reporting procedures.

Revenue Management Consultation

This is a hands on programme to work with every department involved in formulating, implementing and managing the revenue management strategy. We implant a spreadsheet tool, modified to your specific situation, assist in structuring the revenue management process and follow-up with a series of regular conference calls to guarantee your success!

Carol Verret Consulting and Training is a full service company specializing in consulting and training tools you can use in the areas of hotel sales, hotel revenue management and customer service. We work internationally and domestically to provide training and consulting solutions with a demonstrable ROI.

- *Sales and Management Coaching* Ideal for hotel properties who want to develop their management staff in sales and/or leadership skills including hotel revenue management.
- *Sales Seminars, Revenue Management Seminars and Customer Service Seminars*: Sales training and customer service training seminars are tailored programmes with a guaranteed shelf life! Hotel Sales training, leadership, management training and customer service seminars that produce results with reinforcement. We work on strategy, cold calling, qualifying and closing techniques.
- *Consulting—Revenue Management Consultations, Hotel Sales Consulting, Customer Service Consulting* and *Human Resources Consulting* to bring your organization results you can measure. Market Analysis, Property Positioning, Customer Service, Recommendations, Strategies, Sales Plans and on-going support. Do you know how to boost your property's market share? Carol Verret's proven strategies will help you drive hotel sales.
- *Web Casts*: Real time online "Training Bytes" to acquire new or refresh current hotel sales skills. It is our mission to provide the hotel industry with training that is not only useful but also cost effective.
- *Online Training Modules*: Real training—the tools you need when YOU want them. Offered in partnership with HotelTraining.com, these are self-paced sales training modules that include assessments of the skills acquired to guarantee ROI on this training investment.

- *SalesCallCheck*: Sales department mystery shops with immediate audio and written feedback to assess how well you are handling the business.
- *Articles*: Carol Verret has been published in publications as diverse as Hotel Online, Asian Hospitality, Hotel Resource, Hospitality Upgrade among others. She is even featured in a new textbook for hospitality students. Click here to see the archive of her articles —the latest trends that you need to know! ResultsWoW Article News Feeds.
- *Website Development, Positioning and CRM Solutions*: Ideal for independent properties who cannot afford to be without a dynamic Internet presence.

V. International Hotel and Resort Management

MSc/PGDip/PGCert

This MSc in Hotel and Tourism Marketing Management provides an opportunity for honours graduates with hotel, tourism, marketing and management bachelor's degrees, and a minimum one year's relevant work experience, to study at master's level. The focus of your studies will be on marketing management in the international hotel and tourism industry. We recruit students from all around the world, and this creates an exciting multicultural study environment. This programme has three flexible study modes: full-time and sandwich for all students and part-time for British and European Union students.

Our aim is to provide you with intellectual and professional development, and to develop your awareness of culture from multiple perspectives; these are essential qualities for effective international hotel and tourism management. There are options to specialise in several subjects including named awards in financial management, marketing or human resources. You will learn about approaches to management decision-making, critical evaluation, reflective practice and strategic and tactical analysis to solve international business problems in the hospitality and tourism industry.

Hospitality and tourism education at Oxford Brookes University Business School has an excellent international reputation for quality and innovation in learning and teaching. Indeed, leading hospitality and tourism organizations visit the campus to recruit students; and our dedicated careers service and master's sandwich mode of study provide graduates with accelerated career opportunities.

Teaching, Learning and Assessment

The Oxford Brookes innovative learning experience on this MSc includes theatre role-plays in Strategic Management Accounting; creativity in hotel and resort brand design in Marketing Across Cultures; strong links between the Marketing Across Cultures and International Human Resource Management modules; building your own live-case study on a hospitality or tourism company in Strategic Management; and researching/writing an academic journal article in the Contemporary Issues module. Tutors involved in the programme are internationally renowned for their research and consultancy activities, and their excellent links with the hotel and tourism industry. They bring this expertise into the classroom to inform you of contemporary developments taking place in hospitality. Learning and teaching is very much student-centred, participative and interactive. You will take part in workshops, seminars, lectures, theatre role-plays, case study analysis and one-to-one tutorials. The full-time mode involves approximately 15 hours of staff contact time per week, but in addition there is a significant amount of independent and group study time. You will therefore be expected to take a great deal of responsibility for your own learning and to manage your time effectively. Assessment is based predominantly on individual coursework and the dissertation.

Course Content

The following modules build upon your previous learning and work experience to enable you to develop a deeper understanding of the complexity of international hotel and resort management in today's turbulent tourism environment:

Strategic Management Accounting focuses on the use of financial information for managerial decision-making in the international hotel and resort industry. The content includes an exploration of key financial issues, an appraisal of financial techniques and current developments applicable to managerial decision-making. In a small group with other international students you will devise a theatre role-play to explain a current financial topic (to your fellow students).

International Human Resource Management enables you to assess the international hotel and tourism environment so that you can make judgements about the most appropriate human resource management approaches to adopt in different situations. It also aims to increase your awareness of issues that need to be considered when companies decide to expand beyond their domestic market. You will learn how to develop a human resource strategy that supports your chosen market entry strategy for a hospitality company's expansion into a new country. You will also be introduced to a range of practical approaches for the management of people in contemporary organizations.

Marketing Across Cultures introduces you to the concept of marketing within an international hotel and resort context. It provides you with conceptual frameworks to analyse the strategies of international hotel and resort companies. A key feature of the module is the emphasis on the cultural differences and similarities that international hospitality/resort operators have to understand if they are to develop effective global marketing strategies. Working in groups, you will carry out a non-assessed comparative research exercise into a country and market sector from a hotel/restaurant/resort marketing perspective. Your individual assignment involves a country market analysis and market entry strategy for a British hospitality brand's international expansion programme—and you design your own brand!

Strategic Management in International Tourism Firms: As strategic management is, by nature, inter-disciplinary, this module aims to integrate the knowledge you have gained about aspects of the management of hotel and tourism products/services from modules taken in the first semester. In a team you will research the historic and current business context of one sector of the international tourism industry and then individually you will build a case study for one of the leading companies in your sector.

Finally, you will make recommendations for future strategy at executive board level. It is now widely recognised that an international manager must be more than operationally driven; indeed today's international manager must also be a strategic thinker in order to achieve the best performance results for an organisation on a worldwide basis. This module helps you to develop the ability to think strategically.

Contemporary Issues in International Hospitality and Tourism Management provides you with the opportunity to develop a research specialism in climate change, entrepreneurship, environmental issues, finance, human resources, marketing, or the Internet as applied to the international hospitality and resort sector, or you can choose another contemporary topic from a wide choice of options. In this module you will research a contemporary thematic area, critically analyse the literature and theory, and write an article suitable for publication in an academic journal. In undertaking this module you will work on your own with the support of an expert tutor.

One elective: You can choose one elective from a choice of hospitality, tourism or business modules including Destination and Event Development, Interactive Skills in a Cross-cultural Context, or Internet Strategies for Tourism Distribution. Other electives will also be available.

Research Methods and Dissertation provides you with an introduction to research methods so that you are aware of the approaches, methodologies and resources available for your dissertation. The module enables you to design a research project that will ensure that you generate the information required to write the dissertation. You will develop the ability to critically review literature, to identify the gaps in knowledge and develop relevant research skills to facilitate data collection, analysis, interpretation, presentation and writing. The 20,000-word dissertation provides you with the opportunity to demonstrate what you have learned and what you can do, and shows whether you have the ability to work independently. You choose the management topic which you wish to study—this can be the same topic as your Contemporary Issues module or a different subject area.

The **sandwich mode** comprises one year of full-time MSc taught study and one year of full-time, supervised work experience. You have two options:

You can join the programme in January and take the Introduction to Work module. This provides 24 weeks of supervised work experience at an Operative level in Oxford before starting the MSc taught component in September. You would then complete your year's work experience by taking the Manager in Development module after finishing the taught part of the programme.

You can take all of your work experience after studying on the MSc taught component. The sandwich mode of study provides paid, supervised work experience to support your academic studies with a suitable international hospitality and tourism employer, and you carry out an assessed project for the company.

To find out more about this course, please visit the Business School's website.

Quality

The reputation of the Business School is underpinned through membership of and programme accreditations received from the Association of MBAs, the Association of Business Schools, and professional associations such as the Chartered Institute of Personnel and Development, and the European Foundation for Management Development. The Business School is, therefore, widely regarded as one of the best within its peer group.

The Business School's programmes benefit from rigorous quality assurance procedures and regularly receive excellent feedback from external examiners, employers, students and professional bodies. In 2005 Business and Management achieved 'Broad Confidence', the best possible result, in the discipline audit trail as part of the Quality Assurance Agency Institutional Audit.

Many students who graduate from Business School programmes go on to achieve high status in the industry of their choice.

Our research interests focus on the hospitality and tourism industry and we were recognised in the most recent Research Assessment Exercise (RAE) as 'one of the leading hospitality research groups in the UK'. Our research areas include:

- Strategy, policy and performance of international hotel and resort groups.
- Education, careers and development.
- Diversity management.
- Hospitality marketing.
- Consumer satisfaction in tourism and hospitality.
- Financial management decision making.
- Environmental studies.
- Food studies.

All our lecturers have considerable industry experience and are active consultants/researchers. We publish our research in generic, hospitality and tourism academic journals and we author subject-specific textbooks. We enjoy supervising Ph.D. students, many of whom were students on this master's programme before embarking on their own academic career.

Credits and Modules

Oxford Brookes operates the European Credit Transfer System (ECTS). All postgraduate single modules are equivalent to 10 ECTS credits, double modules to 20 ECTS credits, and treble modules to 30 ECTS credits. A full master's course will carry 90 ECTS credits.

Admission

Entry requirements are normally a very good honours degree in hotel, tourism and management (or equivalent) plus at least one year's work experience in the hotel and tourism industry. Entry will also be subject to two satisfactory references (one of these must be an academic reference). Applicants who have limited work experience in the hotel and tourism industry can join the sandwich mode and undertake the Introduction to Work module, which starts in January each year.

If English is not your first language you will need to demonstrate that your level of English is appropriate for study at postgraduate level. In addition to the academic entry qualifications, applicants must have British Council IELTS minimum level 6.5 overall with a minimum level 6 in reading, speaking, understanding and writing, or an equivalent English language qualification acceptable to the University, for example a TOEFL score of 575 or above (paper-based), or 233 or above (computer-based), or 90 or above (Internet-based).

How to Apply

You apply for this course **directly to the University** website (http://www.brookes.ac.uk/studing/applications/direct).

Conditions of Acceptance

When you accept our offer you agree to the conditions of acceptance. You should therefore read those conditions before accepting the offer.

Chapter 4

Hotel Accounting Services, Software and ID Badges

HOTEL ACCOUNTANCY

Accountancy (profession) or *accounting* (methodology) is the measurement, statement or provision of assurance about financial information primarily used by managers, investors, tax authorities and other decision makers to make resource allocation decisions within companies, organizations, and public agencies. The terms derive from the use of financial accounts.

Accounting is the discipline of measuring, communicating and interpreting financial activity. Accounting is also widely referred to as the "language of business".

Financial accounting is one branch of accounting and historically has involved processes by which financial information about a business is recorded, classified, summarised, interpreted, and communicated; for public companies, this information is generally publicly-accessible. By contrast management accounting information is used within an organization and is usually confidential and accessible only to a small group, mostly decision-makers. Tax Accounting is the accounting needed to comply with jurisdictional tax regulations.

Practitioners of accountancy are known as *accountants*. There are many professional bodies for accountants throughout the world. Many allow their members to use titles indicating their membership or qualification level. Examples are Chartered Certified Accountant (ACCA or FCCA), Chartered Accountant (FCA, CA or ACA), Management Accountant (ACMA, FCMA or

AICWA), Certified Public Accountant (CPA) and Certified General Accountant (CGA or FCGA).

Auditing is a related but separate discipline, with two sub-disciplines: internal auditing and external auditing. External auditing is the process whereby an independent auditor examines an organization's financial statements and accounting records in order to express an opinion as to the truth and fairness of the statements and the accountant's adherence to Generally Accepted Accounting Principles (GAAP), or International Financial Reporting Standards (IFRS), in all material respects. Internal auditing aims at providing information for management usage, and is typically carried out by auditors employed by the company, and sometimes by external service providers.

Accounting/accountancy attempts to create accurate financial reports that are useful to managers, regulators, and other stakeholders such as shareholders, creditors, or owners. The day-to-day record-keeping involved in this process is known as book-keeping.

Accounting scholarship is the academic discipline which studies accounting/accountancy.

Modern Accounting/Accountancy

Accounting is the process of identifying, measuring and communicating economic information so a user of the information may make informed economic judgements and decisions based on it.

Accounting is the degree of measurement of financial transactions which are transfers of legal property rights made under contractual relationships. Non-financial transactions are specifically excluded due to conservatism and materiality principles.

At the heart of modern financial accounting is the double-entry book-keeping system. This system involves making at least two entries for every transaction: a debit in one account, and a corresponding credit in another account. The sum of all debits should always equal the sum of all credits, providing a simple way to check for errors. This system was first used in medieval Europe, although claims have been made that the system dates back to Ancient Rome or Greece.

According to critics of standard accounting practices, it has changed little since. Accounting reform measures of some kind have been taken in each generation to attempt to keep book-keeping relevant to capital assets or production capacity. However, these have not changed the basic principles, which are supposed to be independent of economics as such. In recent times, the divergence of accounting from economic principles has resulted in controversial reforms to make financial reports more indicative of economic reality.

History of Accounting

Early History

Accountancy's infancy dates back to the earliest days of human agriculture and civilization (the Sumerians in Mesopotamia), when the need to maintain accurate records of the quantities and relative values of agricultural products first arose. Simple accounting is mentioned in the Christian Bible (New Testament) in the Book of Matthew, in the Parable of the Talents. The Islamic Quran also mentions simple accounting for trade and credit arrangements).

Twelfth-century A.D. Arab writer Ibn Taymiyyah mentioned in his book *Hisba* (literally, "verification" or "calculation") detailed accounting systems used by Muslims as early as in the mid-seventh century A.D. These accounting practices were influenced by the Roman and the Persian civilizations that Muslims interacted with the most detailed example Ibn Taymiyyah provides of a complex governmental accounting system is the Divan of Umar, the second Caliph of Islam, in which all revenues and disbursements were recorded. The Divan of Umar has been described in detail by various Islamic historians and was used by Muslim rulers in the Middle East with modifications and enhancements until the fall of the Ottoman Empire.

Luca Pacioli and the Birth of Modern Accountancy

Luca Pacioli (1445-1517), also known as Friar Luca dal Borgo, is credited for the "birth" of accounting. His *Summa de arithmetica, geometrica, proportioni et proportionalita* (*Summa on arithmetic, geometry, proportions and proportionality*, Venice 1494), was a textbook for use in the abbaco schools of northern Italy, where the sons of merchants and craftsmen were educated. It was a compendium of the mathematical knowledge of his time, and includes the first printed description of the method of keeping accounts that Venetian merchants used at that time, known as the double-entry accounting system. Although Pacioli codified rather than invented this system, he is widely regarded as the "Father of Accounting". The system he published included most of the accounting cycle as we know it today. He described the use of journals and ledgers, and warned that a person should not go to sleep at night until the debits equalled the credits! His ledger had accounts for assets (including receivables and inventories), liabilities, capital, income, and expenses—the account categories that are reported on an organisation's balance sheet and income statement, respectively. He demonstrated year-end closing entries and proposed that a trial balance be used to prove a balanced ledger. His treatise also touches on a wide range of related topics from accounting ethics to cost accounting.

Post-Pacioli

The first known book in the English language on accounting was published in London, England by John Gouge (or Gough) in 1543. It is described as *A Profitable Treatyce called the Instrument or Boke to learn to know the good order of the kepyng of the famouse reconynge, called in Latin, Dare and Habere, and, in English, debtor and Creditor*.

A short book of instructions was also published in 1588 by John Mellis of Southwark, England, in which he says, "I am but the renuer and reviver of an ancient old copies printed here in London the 14 of August 1543: collected, published, made, and set forth by one Hugh Oldcastle, Schoolmaster, who, as reappeared by his treatise, then taught Arithmetics, and this booke in Saint Ollaves parish in Marko Lane." Mellis refers to the fact that the principle of accounts he explains (which is a simple system of double entry) is "after the former of Venice."

A book described as *The Merchants Mirrour, or directions for the perfect ordering and keeping of his accounts formed by way of*

Debitor and Creditor, after the (so termed) Italian manner, by Richard Dafforne, accountant, published in 1635, contains many references to early books on the science of accountancy. In a chapter in this book, headed "Opinion of Book-keeping's Antiquity," the author states, on the authority of another writer, that the form of book-keeping referred to had then been in use in Italy about two hundred years, "but that the same, or one in many parts very like this, was used in the time of Julius Caesar, and in Rome long before." He gives quotations of Latin book-keeping terms in use in ancient times, and refers to "ex Oratione Ciceronis pro Roscio Comaedo"; and he adds:

> "That the one side of their booke was used for Debitor, the other for Creditor, is manifest in a certain place, *Naturalis Historiae Plinii*, lib. 2, cap. 7, where he, speaking of Fortune, saith thus:
>
> *Huic Omnia Expensa.*
> *Huic Omnia Feruntur accepta et in tota Ratione mortalium sola.*
> *Utramque Paginam facit."*

An early Dutch writer appears to have suggested that double-entry book-keeping was even in existence among the Greeks, pointing to scientific accountancy having been invented in remote times.

There were several editions of Richard Dafforne's book—the second edition in 1636, the third in 1656, and another in 1684. The book is a very complete treatise on scientific accountancy, beautifully prepared and containing elaborate explanations. The numerous editions tend to prove that the science was highly appreciated in the 17th century. From this time on, there has been a continuous supply of literature on the subject, many of the authors styling themselves accountants and teachers of the art, and thus proving that the professional accountant was then known and employed.

Accountancy Qualifications and Regulation

The expectations for qualification in the profession of accounting vary between different jurisdictions and countries.

Accountants may be certified by a variety of organizations or bodies, such as the Association of Accounting Technicians (AAT), British qualified accountancy bodies including the Chartered Institute of Management Accountants (CIMA), Association of Chartered Certified Accountants (ACCA) and Institute of Chartered Accountants, and are recognised by titles such as *Chartered Management Accountant* (ACMA or FCMA) *Chartered Certified Accountant* (ACCA or FCCA) and *Chartered Accountant* (UK, Australia, New Zealand, Canada, India, Pakistan, South Africa, Ghana), *Certified Public Accountant* (Ireland, Japan, US, Singapore, Hong Kong, the Philippines), *Certified Management Accountant* (Canada, U.S.), *Certified General Accountant* (Canada), or *Certified Practicing Accountant* (Australia). Some Commonwealth countries (Australia and Canada) often recognise both the certified and chartered accounting bodies. The majority of "public" accountants in New Zealand and Canada are Chartered Accountants; however, Certified General Accountants are also authorised by legislation to practice public accounting and auditing in all Canadian provinces, except Ontario and Quebec, as of 2005. There is, however, no legal requirement for an accountant to be a paid-up member of one of the many Institutes and other bodies which are effectively a form of professional trade union. Unlike the Law Society, which can legally stop a solicitor from practicing, accountancy institutes do not have such authority. However, auditors are regulated.

The "Big Four" Accountancy Firms

The "Big Four auditors" are the largest multinational accountancy firms.

- PricewaterhouseCoopers.
- Ernst and Young.
- KPMG.
- Deloitte Touche Tohmatsu.

These firms are associations of the partnerships in each country rather than having the classical structure of holding company and subsidiaries, but each has an international 'umbrella' organization for coordination (technically known as a Swiss Verein).

Before the Enron and other accounting scandals in the United States, there were five large firms and were called the Big Five: Arthur Andersen, PricewaterhouseCoopers, KPMG, Deloitte Touche Tohmatsu and Ernst and Young.

On June 15, 2002, Arthur Andersen was convicted (later overturned) of obstruction of justice for shredding documents related to its audit of Enron. Nancy Temple (Andersen Legal Dept.) and David Duncan (Lead Partner for the Enron account) were cited as the responsible managers in this scandal as they had given the order to shred relevant documents. Since the U.S. Securities and Exchange Commission does not allow convicted felons to audit public companies, the firm agreed to surrender its licenses and its right to practice before the SEC on August 31, 2002. A plurality of Arthur Andersen joined KPMG in the US and Deloitte and Touche outside of the US. Historically, there had also been groupings referred to as the "Big Six" (Arthur Andersen, plus Coopers and Lybrand before its merger with Price Waterhouse) and the "Big Eight" (Ernst and Young prior to their merger were Ernst and Whinney and Arthur Young and Deloitte and Touche was formed by the merger of Deloitte, Haskins and Sells with the firm Touche Ross).

Enron turned out to be only the first of a series of accounting scandals that enveloped the accounting industry in 2002.

This is likely to have far-reaching consequences for the U.S. accounting industry. Application of International Accounting Standards originating in International Accounting Standards Board headquartered in London and bearing more resemblance to UK than current US practices is often advocated by those who note the relative stability of the UK accounting system (which reformed itself after scandals in the late 1980s and early 1990s). Accounting reform of a far more comprehensive sort is advocated by those who see issues with capitalism or economics, and seek ecological or social accountability.

Bodies and Organizations

Accounting Standard-Setting Bodies

- International

- International Federation of Accountants.
- International Accounting Standards Board.

- United States
  - Financial Accounting Standards Board (FASB).
  - AICPA Accounting Principles Board (APB).
  - AICPA Committee on Accounting Procedure.
  - American Institute of Certified Public Accountants (AICPA).
  - U.S. Securities and Exchange Commission.
  - Governmental Accounting Standards Board (GASB).
  - Federal Accounting Standards Advisory Board (FASAB).

Other Countries (Specific)

Germany

- Accounting Standards Committee of Germany (ASCG, in German: DRSC) .

Australia

- Institute of Chartered Accountants in Australia.

Canada

- Accounting Standards Board "AcSB".

Ghana

- Institute of Chartered Accountants of Ghana.

Hong Kong (see Accountancy in Hong Kong)

- Hong Kong Institute of Certified Public Accountants (HKICPA) [formerly known as Hong Kong Society of Accountants (HKSA)].

India

- Institute of Chartered Accountants of India.

Malaysia

- Malaysian Accounting Standards Board.
- Malaysian Institute of Accountants.

Nigeria

- Institute of Chartered Accountants of Nigeria (ICAN).

New Zealand

- Accounting Standards Review Board.
- New Zealand Institute of Chartered Accountants.

Ireland

- Institute of Chartered Accountants in Ireland.

South Africa

- South African Institute of Chartered Accountants (SAICA).

United Kingdom

- Accounting Standards Board.

Iran

- Accounting Standards Board.

Pakistan

- Institute of Chartered Accountants of Pakistan (ICAP).

Professional Organizations

- American Institute of Certified Public Accountants (AICPA).
- Association of Accounting Technicians (AAT).
- Association of Chartered Certified Accountants (ACCA).
- Association of National Accountants of Nigeria (ANAN).
- Canadian Institute of Chartered Accountants (CICA).
- Certified General Accountants Association of Canada (CGA).
- Guild of Industrial, Commercial and Institutional Accountants, Canada (ICIA).
- Chartered Institute of Cost and Management Accountants (CICMA).
- Chartered Institute of Management Accountants (CIMA).
- Chartered Institute of Public Finance and Accountancy (CIPFA).
- CPA Australia.
- German CPA Society (GCPAS).
- Hong Kong Institute of Certified Public Accountants.
- Institute of Chartered Accountants in Australia.
- Institute of Chartered Accountants in England and Wales (ICAEW).
- Institute of Chartered Accountants in Ireland (ICAI).
- Institute of Chartered Accountants of India.
- Institute of Chartered Accountants of Nigeria (ICAN).
- Institute of Chartered Accountants of Pakistan (ICAP).
- Institute of Chartered Accountants of Scotland (ICAS).
- Institute of Cost and Management Accountants of Pakistan (ICMAP).
- International Federation of Accountants.
- Malaysian Institute of Accountants.
- New Zealand Institute of Chartered Accountants.
- Ordre des Experts Comptables de Tunisie.
- Philippine Institute of Certified Public Accountants.
- South African Institute of Chartered Accountants (SAICA).

Government Agencies

Government agencies enforce the securities laws. Public companies must file financial reports with these government agencies.

United States

- U.S. Securities and Exchange Commission (SEC) (for public companies).
- Federal Reserve (for banks).

Germany

- German Federal Financial Supervisory Authority (BaFin).

India

- Reserve Bank of India (for banks).
- Securities and Exchange Board of India (SEBI) (for public companies).

Pakistan

- State Bank of Pakistan (for Banks).
- Securities and Exchange Commission of Pakistan (for Public Companies including Banks).

Oversight Boards (Regulators for the Accounting Industry)

Oversight boards are new, private-sector non-profit organizations that were set up after the Enron scandal to oversee the auditors of public companies.

United States

- Public Company Accounting Oversight Board—public companies.

Germany

- German Auditor Oversight Commission (AOC, in German: APAK).

Auditing Standards-Setting Bodies

International

- International Auditing and Assurance Standards Board.

United States

- Public Company Accounting Oversight Board—public companies.
- American Institute of Certified Public Accountants—general.
- Government Accountability Office—recipients of federal grants.
- Information Systems Audit and Control Association (ISACA) (Information System Auditing Guideline).

Germany

- German Institute of Certified Public Accountants (IDW).

Australia

- AUASB—Auditing and Assurance Standards Board.

Hong Kong (see Accountancy in Hong Kong)

- Hong Kong Institute of Certified Public Accountants (HKICPA) [formerly known as Hong Kong Society of Accountants (HKSA)].

South Africa

- Public Accountants and Auditors Board-public companies.

United Kingdom

- Auditing Practices Board.

India

- Auditing and Assurance Standards Board.

Pakistan

- Institute of Chartered Accountants of Pakistan.

Size of market

United Kingdom

According to *Accountancy Age's* 2005 league table, fee income amongst the Top 50 accounting firms in the UK rose from £6.3bn to £7.0bn. This followed two successive years in which fee income had declined, largely a result of the sale by some of the larger firms of their consultancy arms. As detailed in the next section, fee income in most business areas - audit, tax, corporate finance and consultancy - rose in the 2005 survey, with insolvency and wealth management being the only segments where revenue fell.

Price water house Coopers remains the largest firm with fee income totaling £1,780m followed by Deloitte (£1,350m), KPMG (£1,066m) and Ernst & Young (£945m). The combined revenue of the Big Fourth accounted for £5.0bn, 72% of the fee income of the Top 50, down from 78-79% in the years up to the 2002 survey and the third year in succession a decline in their share has occurred (Chart 1). Ernst & Young's fee income is the smallest of the largest four firms, but still over three times that of the next largest firm, Grant Thornton. The amount of fee income tapers off amongst the mid-tier firms so that in total there were only 25 firms that each generated more than £15m of revenue in the 2005 survey.

Topics in accounting

See list of accounting for complete listing.

Standards

- International Financial Reporting Standards (IFRS), formerly known as International Accounting Standards (IAS).
- United States generally accepted accounting principles.
- German HGB Accounting Standard.
- United Kingdom generally accepted accounting principles.
- Hong Kong

Auditing

- Assurance services.
- Audit.
- Information technology audit.
- Internal audit.

Accountancy Methods and Fields

- Lean accounting.
- Topics in accounting.
- See list of accounting topics for complete listing.
- Cost accounting.
- Cash-basis and accrual-basis accounting.
- Financial accountancy.
- Fund accounting.
- Internal and external accountancy.

- Management accounting.
- Project accounting.
- Positive accounting.
- Environmental accounting.
- Tax accounting.

Accounting Principles

Accounting principles, rules of conduct and action are described by various terms such as concepts, conventions, tenets, assumptions, axioms and postulates.

Accounting Concepts

- Entity concept.
- Dual aspect concept.
- Going concern concept.
- Accounting period concept.
- Money measurement concept.
- Historical cost concept.
- Periodic matching of cost and revenue concept.
- Verifiable objective evidence concept.
- Realisation concept.
- Accounting methods (includes a discussion on the concept of accruals).
- Understandability.
- Relevance.
- Reliability.
- Comparability.
- Accrual.

Accounting Conventions

- Convention of disclosure.
- Convention of materiality.
- Convention of consistency.
- Convention of conservatism.

Use of computers in accountancy

- Accounting software.
- Databases
- Online Office This allows accounts to be maintained in an online environment.
- spreadsheet programs.
- XBRL.

Types of Accountancy

The following list is intended to give some idea of the breadth and scope of the accountancy profession:

- Lean accounting.
- Auditing.
- Book keeping.
- Chartered accountant.
- Cost accounting.
- Management accounting.
- Financial accounting.
- Forensic accounting.
- Taxation advice.
- Public accountancy.
- Private accountancy.
- Internal accountancy.
- External accountancy.

SALES (ACCOUNTING)

In book-keeping, accounting, and finance, *sales* are operating revenues earned by a company when it sells its products. Sales are reported directly on the income statement as *Sales* or *Net Sales.*

In financial ratios that use income statement sales values, "sales" refers to net sales, not gross sales.

Revenue is earned when goods are delivered or services are rendered. The term sales in a marketing, advertising or a general business context often refers to a contract in which a buyer has agreed to purchase some products at a set time in the future. From an accounting standpoint, sales do not occur until the product is delivered. "Outstanding orders" refers to sales orders that have not been filled.

General Journal

Date	*Description of Entry*	*Debit*	*Credit*
7-7	Cash	200.00	
	Sales		200.00
	Sell 10 books at 20% discount		
7-10	Accounts receivable	125.00	
	Services		125.00
	Consulting fee		

A sale is a transfer of property for money or credit. In double-entry book-keeping, a sale of merchandise is recorded in the general journal as a debit to cash or accounts receivable and a credit to the sales account. The amount recorded is the actual monetary value of the transaction, not the list price of the merchandise. A discount from list price might be noted if it applies to the sale.

Fees for services are recorded separately from sales of merchandise, but the book-keeping transactions for recording "sales" of services are similar to those for recording sales of tangible goods.

Gross Sales and Net Sales

General Journal—Merchandise Return Example

Date	*Description of Entry*	*Debit*	*Credit*
8-7	Sales Returns and Allowances	20.00	
	Accounts Receivable		20.00
	Full credit for customer return of merchandise purchased on account		
8-7	Inventory	20.00	
	Cost of Goods Sold		20.00
	Restore returned merchandise to inventory		

Gross sales are the sum of all sales during a time period. Net sales are gross sales minus sales returns, sales allowances, and sales discounts. Gross sales do not normally appear on an income statement. The sales figures reported on an income statement are net sales.

- ❖ Sales returns are refunds to customers for returned merchandise.
- ❖ Sales allowances are reductions in sales price for merchandise with minor defects, the allowance agreed upon *after* the customer has purchased the merchandise.
- ❖ Sales discounts are reduced payments from the customer based on invoice payment terms such as 2/10, n/30 (2% discount if paid within 10 days, net invoice total due in 30 days).

Sales Returns and Allowances and Sales Discounts are contra-revenue accounts.

General Journal—Sales Discount Example

Date	*Description of Entry*	*Debit*	*Credit*
9-1	Accounts Receivable (Customer A)	500.00	
	Sales		500.00
	Merchandise sale on account, terms 2/10, n/30		
9-7	Cash	490.00	
	Sales Discounts	10.00	
	Accounts Receivable (Customer A)		500.00
	A/R paid by Customer A, taking a 2% discount		

Revenue or *Sales* reported on the income statement are net sales after deducting Sales Returns and Allowances and Sales Discounts.

Revenue		
Sales		$2,000.00
Less Sales returns and allowances	$20.00	
Sales discounts	$10.00	$30.00
Net sales		$1,970.00

HOSPITALITY ACCOUNTING SERVICES, INC: A CASE STUDY

Hospitality accounting services is a multi-faceted company that provides hotel accounting and internal control auditing, data archiving and report automation systems and hotel information systems consulting. It is Hospitality Accounting Services's goal to provide services that enhance the accuracy and efficiency of hospitality information systems and will create a positive, long-term financial impact. The accounting, book-keeping, internal control auditing, contracted Controller solutions, and Expert Witnessing. Our consulting services provide experienced hospitality specialists who will add value to your accounting process with revenue enhancement and cost containment recommendations.

Outsourcing hotel accounting functions has been a standard practice with the evolution external companies processing hotel payrolls. Today, the advantages with outsourcing hotel accounting functions are becoming more apparent. Hospitality Accounting Services, Inc.'s clients range from International full-service hotels, resorts, as well limited-service hotel management companies. We are able to customize our services to meet your needs. We specialize in the hotel internal audit process and adding expertise and value to the accounting process.

Hospitality Accounting Services, Inc. takes pride in our mission statement that "Hospitality Accounting Services, Inc. provides professional hotel accounting services that increase expertise and value to our clients' accounting process and is the hotel industry's premier accounting service."

Hotel Accounting, Internal Control Auditing and Business Information Systems

Hospitality Accounting Services, Inc. (www.hotel-accounting.com) is a multi-faceted company that provides hotel accounting and internal control auditing, data archiving and report automation systems and hotel information systems consulting. It is Hospitality Accounting Services' mission to provide services that enhance the accuracy and efficiency of hospitality information systems that will create a positive, long-term financial impact. The accounting and internal control auditing services provide experienced hospitality specialists who will add value to the auditing process with revenue enhancement and cost containment recommendations.

The archiving and report automation system services offer cost effective approaches leading to business intelligence systems that strategically utilizes archived information. The archiving system, Report Automation System (R.A.S.), provides a short-term pay back period with future annual savings. In addition, R.A.S. software provides the unique technology enabling a host computer to archive information from different hotel systems (*i.e.* PMS, POS, Payroll, Catering and Sales, Human Resources, Telephone, Engineering, and back office Accounting) and reformat new reports from the archived data. These newly formatted reports would be automated and could be sent to remote sites via e-mail, internet, or company WAN. R.A.S. can be upgraded to interface with multi-dimensional tools to create an Business Intelligence System. Overall, the R.A.S. technology allows a hotel or hotel company to cost justify upgrading their information systems by investing in a cost saving strategy that offers a "win-win" opportunity.

Accounting Services

- Our services provide the hospitality accounting expertise to perform accounting and internal control audits.

Consulting Services

- Consulting services providing expertise to maximize hotel business systems efficiency and effectiveness.
- Consulting services to minimize fraud, theft, or embezzlement of funds.
- Consulting services to determine revenue enhancements and cost containment opportunities.
- Software systems consulting ranging from cost effective archiving (storage) of data, report automation, report

data mining capabilities, and business intelligence systems.

C.P.A. firms have demonstrated over the years that their main focus is auditing financial statements. The financial audits or reviews are necessary but expensive. Also, the level of the auditors' hospitality experience is limited and offers little practical knowledge of internal controls. The trend is to reduce the auditing scope and rely on other alternatives.

Regional Controllers and internal audit teams have been very cost efficient alternatives. The growth of our industry has increased the Regional Controller's job scope and responsibilities. The internal audit team can be a costly approach if turnover or the lack of hospitality experience minimize the potential problem-solving benefits an audit can provide. Last, but not least, it has been shown that the integrity of an in-house team performing audits has the potential of being compromised.

The goal of Hospitality Accounting Services is to be the premier accounting service provider in the hospitality industry. The auditing service that we provide will be both cost effective and offer a level of expertise that will add value to your auditing process.

Services

- *Accounting Services*: Our services provide the hospitality accounting expertise to perform hotel accounting and internal control audits.
- *Consulting Services*
    - Consulting services providing expertise to maximize hotel business systems efficiency and effectiveness.
    - Consulting services to assist in fraud and embezzlement situations.
    - Consulting services to determine revenue enhancements and cost containment opportunities.
    - Software systems consulting ranging from cost effective archiving (storage) of data, report automation,

report data mining capabilities, and business intelligence systems.

Hospitality Accounting Services, Inc. presents attractive alternatives to hotel owners and hotel management companies. We believe, our hotel accounting staff combined with today's technology offers reliable expertise and cost savings opportunities. Today, technology advances have successfully afforded other businesses an opportunity to concentrate on their core services. The hospitality industry trends are similiar. Hotels are automating or outsourcing administrative tasks and focusing on their major areas of concern: service, product, and guest satisfaction. The opportunity to gain expertise in the accounting process and minimize the software, hardware, and staffing costs make our accounting options a "win-win" solution for the hotel industry.

The goal of Hospitality Accounting Services, Inc. is to be the premier accounting service provider in the hospitality industry. The accounting services that we provide will be both cost effective and offer a level of expertise that will add value to your accounting process.

Services: Audit Outline

1. Executive review,
2. Cash-general ledger,
3. Accounts receivable,
4. Other assets,
5. Accounts payable,
6. Tax liabilities,
7. Payroll liabilities,
8. Auditing,
9. Purchasing,
10. Receiving,
11. Storeroom,
12. Payroll,
13. Security, and
14. General comments.

Systems

Hospitality Accounting Services, Inc. would like to share several systems links that specialize in accounting and hospitality services respectively. We would encourage you to use this site as a systems resource link to research the options presently available.

- Accounting Systems—AccountingNet.
- Accounting Systems—Excelco.
- Archiving and Report Automation Systems (R.A.S.)—DB Technology, Inc.
- Data Mining Siftware—KD Nuggets .
- Hospitality Systems—Hospitality Index.
- Intelligence Systems—G6G Directory of Intelligent Software.
- OLAP SYSTEMS—Alta Plana.
- Hardware, Software, and Operating Systems—The Ultimate Industry Connection—James Lumber and Ace Hardware.
- Hardware Systems—Tom's Hardware Guide.
- Software Systems—Accounting Top 100 Software Products-1998-Accounting Today.
- Year 2000 Systems—Year 2000 Info Centre.

HOTEL COMPUTERS AND SERVICES, INC: A CASE STUDY OF ACCOUNTING SOFTWARE

Hotel Computers has been providing *INNtime* customized software to the hospitality industry since 1982.

We provide a full featured accounting package specifically designed for the hospitality industry. All modules including general ledger, accounts payable, accounts receivable and payroll are multi-property and multi-user with a security system that provides encrypted password levels by task.

INNtime is currently installed in as few as 46 rooms to over 6300 rooms for a hotel management company.

The system is very, very user friendly and reliable. The reason our customers choose us and stay with us is because our employees who write and install the system are the same employees who support it.

We have worked in hotels and we understand the challenges. We provide real help, everyday, 24 x 7 with a 15 minute or less response time.

As we are the developers of the entire *INNtime* product line, we can provide customized programming at a very reasonable cost. We realize that every hotel and management company has special needs and we can and will fulfill those needs.

Product Lines

- INNtime Hospitality Accounting Systems.
- INNtime Hotel Accounting System.

RESTAURANT/HOSPITALITY ACCOUNTING: ID BADGES

Durability and performance and key words we hear over and over when customers ask us about ID badges to use in their Restaurant and Hospitality Accounting systems. These ID badges are used continuously in reader systems to track orders as they are placed by servers. The ID badges must be secure to withstand the increased reader use... the encoding must be accurate or servers will lose confidence in the system.

Card Durability

IDenticard ID badges feature an exclusive wrapped edge; a single piece of tough, protective laminate that actually wraps around your card. It protects your ID badges from delamination... a common cause of card failure in reader systems. We can supply the cards to you fully laminated, ready for immediate issue.

Card Technology

The technology used on your ID badge depends upon the type of card reader you'll select with your system. The most common technologies are magnetic stripe and bar code. Both magnetic stripes and bar codes can be combined on a single card if necessary.

Magnetic Stripe

IDenticard high coercivity magnetic stripes are protected with Magnacote, an exclusive covering that gives superior protection against abrasion and wear for both the stripe and the reader. Unlike other coatings, Magnacote helps keep the reader head close to the magnetic stripe to assure consistently good readings.

IDenticard's half-inch high coercivity stripes allow multiple track encoding. That means your cards can accommodate two or more different encoding sequences on the same magnetic stripe. Our high coercivity coated stripes are rated at 2,750 oersted, virtually eliminating accidental erasures and read errors. The stripe's constant density makes encoding easy. You may encode your cards yourself or order them already encoded from IDenticard.

Bar Code

There was a time when using a bar code system involved applying sticky labels to your ID badges; a time-consuming process of making sure each label was carefully placed in exactly the right spot. With IDenticard, you can say good-bye to messy bar code labels. With our ID badges, you print bar codes directly on the badge. Bar codes print clearly, cleanly and accurately.

Our special bar code software enables you to do the laser-printing yourself. Or we can handle it for you. We'll supply you with fully-laminated, bar coded cards ready for immediate issue.

Reliability

You can rest assured that your IDenticard ID badges will work in your system. We'll test each card in a reader that you supply to us. Lack of confidence in the cards and reader system is the last thing you need during your hectic serving times.

M3 ACCOUNTING SERVICES AND ITS PRODUCTS: A CASE STUDY

Acknowledge is a complete hotel and restaurant accounting package designed for companies with multiple locations. Acknowledge lets you gather and manipulate data, 24/7, using Internet technology.

Innquire is a Web-based data-mining tool that allows managers to write and run their own multi-unit reports with unlimited statistics. Innquire is your warehouse of information that consists of data from your property level Daily Reports. Finally, seamless payroll integration from timecard to paycheck. LaborWatch brings it all together to give you multi-unit reporting of actual hours vs. volume adjusted standards and Benchmark your performance vs. others in the industry.

About M3, What is Hosting?

The Data Centre our Clients News and Press

M3 was created out of one of the oldest and most successful hospitality companies in the industry. This experience, coupled with its software development expertise, has allowed M3 to develop an integrated suite of hospitality products including Acknowledge, Innquire and LabourWatch. These products, utilizing Internet-based technology, allow owners, operators and managers unsurpassed access to the information they need most.

M3 was the first ASP, or Application Service Provider, in the Hospitality industry. Hosting their applications in a professionally managed, centralized data centre allows clients easy access to their information *via* the Internet. Clients do not have to purchase software, rather they access it online. Included in the monthly fee is all of the hardware, software, support, maintenance and upgrades necessary for the client to manage and grow their business. And, there is no contract to sign!

In 1998, M3 became the first company in the world to offer hosted hospitality applications. By the end of 1999, over 75 hotels subscribed to the M3 product suite. For the first time, many corporate executives could view their information online, first thing in the morning, without having to wait on anyone to fax or e-mail information to them, or having a clerk consolidate a report.

It took M3 two years, over $1,000,000, and the advice of countless experts to develop the initial product. Since that time, hundreds of enhancements have been made at no additional cost to our clients.

And the future is bright for M3. Doubling its business in 2000, and again in 2001, M3 has never lost a customer and has never had a price increase. Our system is up 24 x 7, 365 days a year, and we take every step to insure that your data is safe.

Hosting is application software that resides in a professionally managed third-party data centre. The client subscribes to use the application on a monthly basis. Included in the subscription fee are hardware, software, data security and storage, as well as ongoing support, maintenance and upgrades.

Why should you Consider Hosting with M3?

- ❖ Your data is secure and maintained by professionals.
- ❖ Access is available 24 hours a day from anywhere in the world via the Internet.
- ❖ Costs are typically 50 per cent to 75 per cent less than owning and managing your own system.
- ❖ M3 employs technical experts to manage the system for you.
- ❖ No need to purchase expensive equipment and hardware is kept up-to-date at no additional cost.
- ❖ Software enhancements occur frequently at no cost to you!
- ❖ Contracts are not required. Pay as you go, leave without penalty.

The protection of your data is our Number 1 priority. From the hardware we use, to the high level of data encryption, our clients' information is safe.

At M3, we've standardized on enterprise level servers to run our hosted applications and store your data.

Redundancy is the key. M3 has implemented a sophisticated backup scheme that allows our clients' data to be stored multiple times, on multiple servers and storage devices. As an added precaution, all data is stored off site, daily.

Furthermore, we have implemented industry leading firewall solutions and virus protection to guard against unwanted entry into our data centre.

Data Center

The protection of your data is our Number 1 priority. From the hardware we use, to the high level of data encryption, our clients' information is safe.

At M3, we've standardized on enterprise level servers to run our hosted applications and store your data.

Redundancy is the key. M3 has implemented a sophisticated backup scheme that allows our clients' data to be stored multiple times, on multiple servers and storage devices. As an added precaution, all data is stored off site, daily.

Furthermore, we have implemented industry leading firewall solutions and virus protection to guard against unwanted entry into our data center.

M3 Products Acknowledge

Acknowledge Features How it Works Success Stories Screenshots Getting Started

M3 Acknowledge links your Properties and Corporate Office to a common site. Data is entered directly into the system at the property level. This reduces the cost, time, and inefficiency of two or more people handling the same paperwork. Fax machines are no longer needed. Overnight delivery costs are cut and your management team gets immediate, same-day daily reports and on-demand financial reporting including General Ledger, Accounts Payable, Inventory Management and much more.

In an environment of ever-changing conditions, management will spend far less time hunting and gathering information and more time guiding associates and satisfying guests.

Examples

Do you have several partnerships or would you like to review data by region? Run consolidated income statements for any group of properties in minutes.

Does your corporate staff need information from a specific daily report? No need to call the property. You can see the property level daily report on your screen.

When can your corporate accounting staff start work on month end? With Acknowledge, you can start as soon as the hotel completes the daily report. Your monthly journal entries are prepared and ready for review and posting immediately. No more waiting on faxes or e-mails for your monthly information. Your income statement deadlines can be moved up earlier in the month.

Being audited by a state agency or need information for your insurance/workers comp company? With Acknowledge, you can create reports in minutes giving you the specific information you need for one or more properties on the same report.

M3 Product InnQuire

InnQuire Features How it Works Screenshots

M3's data mining tool, InnQuire, is designed to help managers and owners analyze the performance of their company. Based on your Daily Report, you can easily retrieve and compare information for one or more locations. And, the reports you define are available 24 × 7 from anywhere in the world!

Compare brands. Compare divisions. Track occupancy, rates, revenues, labour costs, etc.

M3 Products LabourWatch Payrol Processing

LabourWatch Benchmarking How it Works Success Stories Screenshots Getting Started

M3 LabourWatch is an exclusive Internet-based labour reporting system allowing you to design your own custom reports to manage overtime and labour hours. In addition, it provides a seamless payroll process from time clock to pay check.

As with all M3 products, software and hardware costs (except time clocks) are included in the monthly fee. Conversion and start up fees are minimal.

Monthly fees may be less than you pay today for payroll processing. M3 LabourWatch includes:

- Time and Attendance Software.
- Management Reports.
- Payroll Processing.
- Software Upgrades and Maintenance.
- Data Storage.
- Hardware Upgrades and Maintenance.

But the savings don't stop there. M3 LabourWatch will reduce corporate office labour and technology expenses:

- Save time collecting, calculating and allocating employee hours.
- Apply payroll policies and work rules across your organization.
- Schedule based on forecasted business levels.

Chapter 5

Hotel, Motel and Resort Management: Selected Case Studies

HOTEL MANAGER

A hotel manager or hotelier is a person who handles the everyday function and management of a hotel. Larger hotels often have management teams, instead of individual managers, where each member of the group begins to specialize on a certain area of interest.

Occupational Tasks

Some of the responsibilities of a hotel manager include:

- Organizing and directing the hotel's services—
  - concierge,
  - reception,
  - reservations, and
  - catering.
- Controlling budget and formulating financial plans.
- Promoting the business.
  - marketing,
  - advertising.

- Archiving profits and expenses
- Meeting with customers, contractors and suppliers
- Hiring, training, reviewing and overseeing staff members
- Attending to problems or customer complaints and comments
- Addressing maintenance and upkeep
- Seeing to accommodations
  - furniture.
- Meeting safety, health and licensing regulations
  - security.

HOTEL MANAGEMENT: CASE STUDIES

Hotel Management International

Hotel Management International (HMI) is your premier hotel site selection company. We provide full assistance in hotel search and contract negotiation to corporations and associations for their off-site business meetings and conference at no cost.

HMI understands the need to continually reduce cost allowing your organization to maxim its profitability, which is our basis for conducting an elaborate search of quality hotels to ensure your always get the most out of your travel budget. Ultimately, our success is measured by our clients achieving their goals.

By working with our team of seasoned professionals with diverse and accomplished backgrounds in the hotel and corporate travel industries, you will only be enhancing the hotels experience for your group's event.

Services

- *Hotel Search*: We conduct an extensive search of hotels based on your preferences and criteria.

- *Request for Proposal (RFP)*: The RFP is sent out to national hotel representatives and independent hotels (if applicable) inviting them to submit a bid for the event.
- *Presentation of Findings in Comparison Table*: With the proposals that are received from the individual hotels, we present our findings in a comprehensive spreadsheet so you can compare the benefits of each hotel option.
- *Hotel Options Short Listed—Process of Elimination*: We narrow the list of hotels down to the most favourable by focusing on those that offer the most attractive bundle.
- *Negotiation of Rates and Concessions*: From the desired hotels identified, we proceed to negotiate rates and concessions. You will benefit from important cost savings and additional concessions due to our buying power, expertise in the hotel industry, strong negotiation skills, and preferred relationships with the hotels. You can focus on other aspects of your programme while we do the work for you at no cost.
- *Hotel Selection*: With our guidance, you select the property that best matches your budget and requirements.
- *Acceptance of Contract*: We ensure all the required elements are in the contract before finalizing the booking including clauses that protect your interests and minimize your risk.
- *Ongoing Support*: Your appreciation of our services is our utmost concern. We will facilitate your stay at the hotel by making sure any issues, if they occur, are resolved promptly.
- *Post-Event Feedback*: We discuss with you your group's overall experience at the hotel and can work with you to verify the accuracy of the charges on the invoice before sending it to your accounting office.

HVS/AMERICAN HOSPITALITY MANAGEMENT COMPANY

HVS/American Hospitality Management Company provides hotel management, oversight management, consulting services and special services, including: receivership services, volume purchasing agreements, and redecorating and refurbishing.

Through our expert staff, refined technical resources and thorough operational systems, HVS/American Hospitality Management Company has a proven ability to deliver service and value.

In October 2004, American Hospitality Management Company, which was established on 1988, joined with HVS International. The company provides:

- Hotel, Motel and Resort Management.
- Consulting Services.
- Oversight and Asset Management.
- Receivership Services.
- Technical and Pre-opening Services.

Our staff has the depth of experience to manage your hotels professionally, regardless of their scope or number of rooms. In addition, we are skilled in the design and implementation of viable plans to increase a property's profile and profitability.

HVS/American Hospitality Management Company's has a corporate structure that allows us to focus our attention on your properties and give personalized service to our clients.

Services

HVS/American Hospitality Management Company, established in 1988, provides hotel, motel and resort management, consulting services, oversight and asset management, receivership services, and technical and pre-opening services in all areas of the hospitality industry.

With a staff that has over 85 years of combined experience in the hospitality industry, HVS/American Hospitality Management Company is competent and knowledgeable in providing services that will maximize cash flow and return on investment for any investor, for any type and size of property.

Hotel, Motel and Resort Management

General

With our Management Philosophy as a guide, HVS/American Hospitality Management Company provides Hotel Management Services to a wide variety of hotels in a number of different locations across the United States. As a hotel operator/manager we have the capacity to maximize cash flow and return on investment for your property, thus increasing its value. The following gives you information on how we do it.

Getting to Know the Property

When we take on a property we make an initial property visit during which our goal is to gain a complete understanding of the physical facilities, their condition, the market environment, operating procedures, and existing management personnel. From this point, we are able to formulate and begin to implement the changes that will be necessary to operate the hotel more efficiently and maximize revenues.

Cash Flow Maximization

In addition to maximizing revenues and managing expenses appropriately, this includes regular cash flow forecasting, weekly cash sweeps to concentrating accounts with excess funds automatically invested. We will monitor and help challenge real estate taxes and insurance costs. We will make debt service and other payments for the owner and assist in debt renegotiation.

Business Planning

Proper planning and information is required for a hotel to best reach its operating potential. HVS/American Hospitality Management Company sees to it that a Business Plan is prepared annually for each hotel that we manage. The plan includes details on the hotel's market, capital improvement needs, and operating history. The preparation of the plan involves the use of activity calendars for planning and future monitoring. The information provided will work to support the hotel's marketing plan and operating budget.

Property Visits

Visits to the property occur on both a regularly scheduled and unscheduled follow-up basis for the purpose of inspection, consultations with management personnel, and ongoing operations and marketing reviews. Our quality control process also includes regular visits by anonymous shoppers who use report formats tied to our operating standards. This allows us to see our hotels through a customer experience.

Weekly Reports

We provide weekly reports to owners depending on their needs. Our accounting system allows owners to view financial data at any time using a web-browser. For instance, some owners receive a weekly report detailing month-to-date revenues, occupancy and Average Daily Rate (ADR) for the current month while others simply look at that data over the Internet at convenient times and places of their own choosing.

Volume Purchasing Agreements

Whenever practical, volume-purchasing agreements are negotiated. Many hotels managed by HVS/American Hospitality Management Company are franchised and full advantage is taken of the franchisor purchasing programmes. Additionally, it is sometimes possible to arrange marketing and other hotel operations purchases in conjunction with other hotels we manage. When such arrangements are possible and provide a discount, costs are prorated to the properties benefitted. No fees, commissions or other arrangements are charged or collected to benefit the management company for these services and our contract specifically forbids "Hidden Fees."

Redecorating and Refurbishing

With our knowledge of current trends and products in the hotel and hospitality industry, we are adept in supervising the redecorating and refurbishments of properties. Redecorating and refurbishing work may be done by hotel employees, contractors or design firms, depending on the project's scope. Fees, if any, depend on the scope of the work and the level of our responsibility.

Asset and Oversight Management

Goal

The goal of oversight management is to advise a client on the operations and financial management of a hotel to help maintain or improve its value. The client might be the owner of the property, a lender or other interested party. We work for the client by monitoring the on-site property manager (individual or management company) on a regular basis for operating performance and maintenance of this valuable asset.

Things Change

Many factors influence when a client may be forced to examine market position, financial structure, operating policies or management of a hotel. Competitors with modern technology, aggressive marketing or changing brand affiliations put pressure on owners and lenders to reexamine their situation. Rising remodelling costs make it more important to maintain a hotel or motel at its best. Without good oversight management, the equity and reputation built up over the years may diminish rapidly. More importantly, the value of the property does not achieve its maximum potential so cash returns from either operations or a sale may not reach the owner's goals.

Insurance Worth the Price

Through recommendations to improve the physical facility, increase revenue growth, and provide consistent quality of service, and reviewing the market strategy and expense controls, efforts are made to enhance the value of the asset. The property is visited on a regularly scheduled basis for inspections and consultations with management personnel on ongoing operations, marketing, and the implementation of suggested changes made during previous visits.

Written reports regarding property visits and meetings with corporate and on-site management are submitted as appropriate. Additionally, written comment is provided to the owner as a follow-up on reports from the Operator and their staff. These follow-up reports include an analysis and critique of the financial statements.

Oversight management provides an independent perspective on the hotel and insures owners or lenders that their interests are being addressed.

How We Do it

Maximize the interest level of the operator and productivity levels of the property's staff so as to increase cash flow.

Insure that the physical maintenance and the capital expenditures to improve the property are completed thereby maintaining or improving the physical condition of the hotel.

Assist the owner in developing realistic goals for the property, communicating those to the operator and subsequently encouraging their achievement by reviewing, in detail, the operator's efforts towards achieving those goals.

Technical and Pre-opening Services

General

With HVS/American Hospitality Management Company on board for a property opening or major repositioning, you will be working with hotel management experts that have gone through the hotel development and opening experience a countless number of times. We have the capacity to oversee everything from concept development, site selection, design coordination and contractor selection to the stocking of shelves and obtaining the right equipment, décor, licenses, and staff as well as the organizing of opening events. We can help any investor through the experience of developing and opening any size hotel, motel, or resort.

Professional Input and Opinions

With our knowledge of and background in hotel operations we are able to consult with the architects and designers concerning design criteria, requirements, and layouts of all functioning areas of the hotel. We can also lend our expertise to the development of general themes and concepts and can assist in the selection and preparation of designs for all furnishings, operating equipment, and operating supplies. Additionally, we are able to review and advise schematics, architectural and engineering plans, and specifications for all aspects of a hotel property. With our expertise we are able to make recommendations and advise changes to plans and specifications whenever necessary.

Compliance

As the operator we are able to obtain and maintain all licenses and permits required of the owner. We will assist the owner in understanding and adhering to all applicable laws, rules, regulations, requirements, and ordinances that are pertinent to hotel operation such as employment law and ADA requirements.

Staffing

In assisting with your opening, we can creatively recruit, hire, and effectively train the right people to help you accomplish your goals. Our employment process includes criminal and credit check for all staff followed by detailed orientation and training leading to industry wide certification that contribute to the professionalism and retention of the hotel's staff.

Pre-opening Marketing

Grand opening activities should help to launch your property into the market. HVS/American Hospitality Management

Company's sales and marketing experience is a great asset in this endeavour. As operator we can coordinate all grand opening activities, sales efforts, advertising, and promotion necessary for the opening of a property. The scope and style of the opening activities need to be appropriate for the hotel itself, the community and the targetted demand generators/markets.

Banking, Reporting and Record-keeping

We are able, on behalf of the owner, to deposit and disburse the appropriate monies and keep record of the monies utilized in the development of the property. Every month, we will provide the appropriate detailed financial statements, schedules and progress reports. In addition, we will maintain the appropriate records related to development.

Planning and Progress Monitoring

Microsoft Project software helps us manage schedules and resources, collaborate on projects, and analyze project information. When projects are larger, more complex and involve more people and companies we can use Microsoft Project Server which allows Internet access for all those involved in managing and carrying out the development or repositioning project

Fees and Staffing

Fees for Technical and Pre-opening services are entirely a function of the level of responsibility and involvement HVS/American Hospitality Management Company assumes. For staffing an appropriate balance is found between current staff and temporary staff and consultants so that our client's resources are used most efficiently.

Receivership Service

Overview

HVS/American Hospitality Management Company has expertise in the management of hotels in transitional and distressed circumstances and has extensive experience being appointed receiver. With our expertise we are able to provide efficient and cost effective Receivership Services for lenders that are preparing to foreclose and sell a property.

Appointment

Our principal officers are well-acquainted with the court proceedings involved in the appointment of a receiver. Our experience gives us the ability to efficiently go through the legal process with our clients including insuring that the all important order appointing a receiver is adequate in its scope and provides the necessary tools for both a smooth transition but also cleaning up unpaid bills and leases.

Takeover

Utilizing our management knowhow and our company's flexible structure, we are able to smoothly take over operation of the property, on very short notice if necessary. When we become receiver, we enter it as we would any hotel we manage. As you would expect, we will be present at the hotel at the time of takeover to become familiar with its operations and implement the necessary changes. The appropriate background checks are performed on all employees and they are rehired and placed on the payroll of an affiliate of ours in order to reduce the investor's associated risk.

Management

We make sure that the assets of the property, both physical and monetary are protected and accounted for. Financial and accounting work for the property is done by experienced staff in our offices. The accounting system that HVS/American Hospitality Management Company utilizes permits our clients to view financial data over the Internet using a web browser, allowing the interested parties to stay up to date with the business of their asset. Additional reports are prepared and submitted as necessary.

Why Us?

HVS/American Hospitality Management Company is able to efficiently develop and execute the necessary hotel business plans that will increase the efficiency and appearance of a hotel. This will help the selected hotel broker show the hotel in the best possible light to prospective buyers. We will work hard to help effectively dispose of the hotel asset.

Usually no Additional Cost

Receivership Services generally cost no more than regular management services for other hotels that HVS/American hospitality company manages. The exception is when extra court appearances are required or when borrowers challenge the Receiver entity on some matter. In that case reasonable hourly rates are charged and all concerned are advised in advance. As Receiver we do retain outside counsel and this is an expense of the Receivership.

Consulting

General Consulting

HVS/American Hospitality Management Company provides consulting services covering a wide range of subjects including operations, marketing and financial structure. We also coordinate consulting assignments with other divisions of HVS international, major international firms and members of the international society of hospitality consultants, with which we enjoy special relationships, so that our clients get the maximum benefit for their dollars invested in consulting.

Operational and Marketing Analysis

We conduct operational and marketing reviews of hotels for the purpose of identifying shortcomings in marketing efforts, operational inefficiencies, service deficiencies which may be inappropriate for that particular hotel, improper and wasteful payroll scheduling and other waste. These reviews are very useful for increasing cash flow, developing workout plans or analyzing budgets and cash flow forecasts for hotels.

Demand Studies, Market Overviews and Impact Analysis

We conduct services for owners finding themselves in situations where they must respond to their franchisor locating an affiliate within the competitive area or for situations where either new construction is underway or a major refurbishing will drastically change the distribution of demand within the market. We also prepare abbreviated Market Overviews and Demand Studies which consist of a five to ten pages report discussing the potential hotel market, how the proposed property should be positioned within it and include estimates of annual Occupancy Percentage and Average Daily Rate. Estimates of operating results over the first five years of operation are prepared. In cases, where a full market demand study is required by a lender from an independent consulting firm, we coordinate and supervise the engagement to insure its accuracy and cost effectiveness.

Litigation Support and Expert Testimony

Our staff is experienced in assisting attorneys with hotel industry information, practices and analysis so as to support litigation involving hotels. That litigation experience includes operations, contract practices, marketing, financial structure, mortgage reviews and financial statement reviews, among others. We have staff who are experienced in both courtroom and administrative hearings.

Fee Structure

Our philosophy regarding our compensation is fundamentally that we make every attempt to create a situation where our clients never question our motivations. We try to align our fee structure to the owner's financial goals.

Management Contracts

We prefer to divide management fees into two parts. The base management fee is intended to cover our basic costs of providing our services. An incentive management fee ties our profitability to the results of our efforts as shown in the profitability of the hotels we manage.

Base Fee

This is usually a percentage of total revenues, or a minimum monthly amount, whichever is greater. The percentage ranges from two to four per cent.

Incentive Fee

Once the owner's financial goals for the hotel are understood and achievable results are agreed to, an incentive management fee is negotiated which relates to those goals.

Consulting and Oversight Management Services

Consulting fees are negotiated on an individual basis depending on the services provided and the time involved. On certain projects, fixed fees are applied while others are on an hourly basis. Hourly fees vary with the level of staff experience necessary and the complexity of the assignment.

Asset Management

Fees are also divided into two parts. The Base Asset Management Fee is intended to cover our basic costs of providing our services. An Incentive Asset Management Fee ties our profitability to the results of our efforts as shown in the profitability of the hotels we manage.

Base Fee

This is usually a flat monthly amount based on the services provided.

Incentive Fee

Once the owner's financial goals for the hotel are understood and achievable results are agreed upon, an Incentive Asset Management Fee is negotiated which relates to those goals and our level of influence over management.

Litigation Support

HVS/American Hospitality Management Company, established in 1988, provides hotel, motel and resort management, consulting services, oversight and asset management, receivership services, and technical and pre-opening services in all areas of the hospitality industry.

With a staff that has over 85 years of combined experience in the hospitality industry, HVS/American Hospitality Management Company is competent and knowledgeable in providing services that will maximize cash flow and return on investment for any investor, for any type and size of property.

Services

HVS Consulting and Valuation Services has one of the most experienced professional staffs, an impeccable worldwide reputation and the highest level of credibility. Thus, hotel projects attract immediate attention when accompanied by an HVS consulting report.

The Hospitality Industry's Challenge

Hotel owners and potential owners must be able to act and plan with confidence when investing in hotel real estate. That can be accomplished only with full knowledge of the real value of the property in question.

They also face the vagaries of a changing market 365 days each year. Doing so without support from experts who understand all the nuances of the hospitality industry could lead to financial disaster.

There is so much knowledge needed to ascertain whether a hotel should be built, bought or sold, and once in operation, how to keep it running smoothly and profitably. Changing markets and variances in neighbourhood and real estate values can cause fluctuations in how a hotel is valued. The most up-to-date and precise information is necessary at all times.

The HVS Client

Our valuation and consulting services are driven by the needs of our clients. Those who come to HVS want information that is highly regarded and accepted by leading lenders, investors, operators and other interested parties. We stand alone in our support for investors and operators who are new to this marketplace, as well as to those who have vast experience in hospitality.

The unique needs of each client are met because we structure our assignments in order to meet your timing needs and all of your other requirements.

Adapting a hotel to changing needs, while at the same time planning for the cyclical nature of the hotel industry, requires having experts on your team who can lead the way in good times, as well as guide you through the difficult periods.

If you need the highest level of credibility from a professional staff that has more experience than any other in the industry, turn to HVS Consulting and Valuation Services.

The HVS Solution

Hospitality valuation services was founded in 1980 to satisfy the demand for strong consultation services and valuation needs. In 1990, the name of the firm was changed to HVS international to combine the historic ties to hospitality valuation services to its global outlook on the hospitality industry. Over the years, the scope of our professional services has expanded to include a wide range of consulting activities.

With a staff of more than 150 professionals, HVS has provided valuation services for more than 10,000 hotels in all 50 states and 60 countries.

Our database of hotel information, combined with broad insight and extensive experience, enables HVS consulting and valuation services to produce well-documented appraisal reports that contain fully supported value conclusions.

Our consultants and appraisers understand the hotel business. Most have degrees in hotel management from top hotel schools, and each has actual hotel operating experience. Our staff has extensive training in real estate and valuation techniques.

The HVS Tools

HVS specializes in the valuation of accommodation facilities and has evaluated thousands of lodging properties of all sizes throughout the world. Our database of hotel investment information, which is the largest in the world, includes information on virtually every major hotel transaction that has taken place in the United States during the past 15 years. We also have a large database of information on international transactions.

HVS Valuation Services has access to thousands of management agreements, franchise contracts, leases, mortgages and other related financial documents. Our databases allow the HVS team to provide thorough documentation for our conclusions.

Our specialized valuation services include:

- Real estate tax assessment appeals and expert court testimony at certiorari proceedings.
- Valuation prior to flotation or public offering of shares.
- Appraisals for condemnation proceedings and related court testimony.
- Expert valuation testimony for foreclosure and bankruptcy proceedings.
- Estate, gift tax and partnership appraisals.
- Quantification of damages from a loss in value.

- ❖ Purchase price allocations among real estate, personal property, and intangibles to establish property tax basis and accounting records.
- ❖ Valuations of hotel management and franchise companies.
- ❖ Valuations of related hospitality facilities, including restaurants, casinos, timeshares and ski resorts.

Because of our professionalism and worldwide reputation for credibility, excellence and thoroughness, our valuation reports hold up under scrutiny and achieve their intended results.

We have a database of information along with broad insight and extensive experience that enables us to produce well-documented consulting reports that contain fully supported recommendations and conclusions.

The staff of HVS Consulting Services continuously monitors every major hotel market and tracks the latest economic trends. The writings, teachings and innovative research at HVS demonstrate our internationally acknowledged expertise. We have published more than 300 articles in leading hotel journals and periodicals.

Our services include:

- ❖ Feasibility studies on income and/or return on investment.
- ❖ Valuations; market value estimates; investment value estimates; and fractional interest valuations.
- ❖ Development consulting and project management.
- ❖ Market audits and promotional strategies.
- ❖ Litigation support and expert testimony.
- ❖ Physical asset assessment.
- ❖ Management contract analysis and negotiation.
- ❖ Operator selection and management company search.
- ❖ Franchise evaluation and selection.
- ❖ Financial damages estimates.
- ❖ Sales and marketing package preparation.
- ❖ Lease reviews and negotiations.
- ❖ Strategic advice and company restructuring.

HOTEL MANAGEMENT: AN OVERVIEW

The Hospitality Industry's Challenge

Hospitality investments in the form of hotels, motels and resorts represent a unique combination of real estate and business investment. Many of the characteristics of retail service establishments are present along with the high capital investment that is common to real estate ownership. Unlike other retail service establishments, the inventory (guestrooms, lounge seats, etc.) has a short shelf life of as little as one hour. Unlike other forms of real estate, rental (lease) periods are daily, however, rental rates can be raised on short notice. Another factor, which is foreign to other forms of real estate, is the management and labour intensiveness of the hospitality industry.

The HVS Client

Investment groups who prefer not to be directly involved in the operation of their hotel investments.

Lenders and special servicers in either the foreclosure process or disposition phase that need receivership and/or management services for transitional or distressed properties. Groups considering purchasing or developing a hotel, motel or resort who want assistance with the process and support coordinating the various disciplines necessary to complete the process.

Law firms seeking the perspective of an owner/operator for litigation support for a wide range of issues associated with buying, owning, selling and operating hotels of various sizes and complexity.

Owners and operators seeking operational or marketing consulting from a hotel operator with a diverse in-depth experience in hotel operations.

Institutional owners who do not have an in-house hotel asset management staff to help develop strategic plans for achieving the investment goal and for coordinating the efforts of the existing management and others over the lifespan of the investment in order to maximize their interest.

The HVS Solution

HVS/American Hospitality Management Company is privileged to have an efficient staff with years of combined experience in the hospitality industry who are competent and knowledgeable in providing services that will maximize cash flow and return on investment for any investor, for any type and size of property.

This same staff, in conjunction with other industry professionals from the HVS International Global Hospitality Consulting Network, where necessary, can bring the unique perspective of an owner/operator with extensive consulting experience to a variety of hotel development projects or consulting and litigation support engagements.

The HVS Tools

For management contract clients we offer reasonable base management fees, a mutually agreeable incentive management fee, and term lengths and cancellation clauses focused on each of our client's needs. Here is a sample of some of our "tools":

- Get to know the property, its staff and market.
- Cash flow maximization by driving revenues and vigorously controlling expenses.
- Business planning with detailed market plans, budgets and capital improvements when appropriate.
- Property visits to assist the management team in carrying out the business plan.
- Periodic reports to keep our corporate staff appraised of progress and areas needing attention.
- Volume purchasing agreements to maintain consistency and cost controls.
- Redecorating and refurbishing as needed to enhance market appeal and operating efficiencies.
- Web-based centralized accounting and accounts payable with ADP payroll systems.
- Human resource procedures that create a sense of belonging while motivating employee teams.

For asset management and operational consulting clients we offer a range of fee structures tailored to each unique situation and focused on the client's goals from the assignment. Our "tools" include, but are not limited to

- ❖ maximize the interest level of the operator and productivity levels of the property's staff so as to increase cash flow.
- ❖ insure that the physical maintenance and the capital expenditures to improve the property are completed thereby maintaining or improving the physical condition of the hotel.
- ❖ assist the owner in developing realistic goals for the property, communicating those to the operator and subsequently encouraging their achievement by reviewing, in detail, the operator's efforts towards achieving those goals.

SALES AND MARKETING SERVICES: AN OVERVIEW

HVS sales and marketing services is ready to strengthen your sales, marketing, public relations and yield management initiatives to maximize your revenue. Our hands-on experience and knowledge has proven particularly valuable for independent hotels who face known brands in their competitive set, as well as for branded hotels which simply do not capitalize on the marketing opportunities provided by their brands or which do not conduct their own proactive marketing.

We can assist during times of renovation, pre-opening, repositioning and when times are steady and strong in order to prepare for a potential downturn period.

And with the power of HVS' understanding of regional markets around the world, we can utilize that competitive strength in your respective marketing efforts. We assist hotel owners and operators with the following sales and marketing communications activities:

- ❖ Reviewing a hotel(s)'s sales and marketing operation and initiatives.
- ❖ Creating a specific sales action plan and strategic marketing plan based on the review and assessment.

- Utilizing the numerous sales and marketing options already provided by your brand, if you carry a flag, and ensure that your efforts meet brand standards.
- Integrating effective web marketing and online efforts into the sales and marketing plan.
- Training appropriate staff in revenue management.
- Assessing, coaching and directing the sales individuals on the hotel's team.
- Developing standard operating procedures by working with all operational departments to insure the guest service levels parallel the marketing promise.
- Developing packages.
- Communicating appropriate messages to targeted market segments through press releases and other professional public relations tactics.
- Reviewing and contributing to a hotel's website for proper search engine optimization and merchandising of packages and specials.
- Assembling a media plan, including e-mailings to boost need periods and overall image.

And this is the start. Our clients can attest to our loyalty, knowledge and teamwork. Client references and some of our successes are shared on www.hvs.com\services\marketing.comm\successstories\. We are known for identifying opportunities as they present themselves so that the hotel doesn't miss a beat. If you commit to the upkeep of the facility, we'll commit to supporting you with your marketing and service—ensuring that your guests will want to return.

May we meet with you to see how we can help you strengthen the return on your hospitality investment?

DRIFTWOOD HOSPITALITY MANAGEMENT

Exceptional Growth and Proven Track Record

Driftwood hospitality management, LLC owns, operates and develops hotels in the U.S., affiliates of the company operate in the Caribbean and Latin America. The company's current portfolio consists of 44 hotels comprising over 8,900 rooms in major resort destinations and top business travel and convention markets in thirteen U.S. states, the Bahamas and Costa Rica.

Our hotel portfolio includes many award-winning franchises of nationally recognized hospitality brands such as Radisson, Wyndham, Crowne Plaza, Sheraton, Hilton, Hampton Inns and Courtyard by Marriott, Holiday Inn Express, Hotel Indigo, Select by Holiday Inn and Doubletree. Driftwood's expertise covers a broad range of lodging options, from mid-size extended-stay and limited service properties, to boutique and full-service resorts featuring bars and restaurants, spas and convention centres.

Driftwood Hospitality Management has a proven track record in all aspects of the hospitality business including Internet distribution and eMarketing, sales and marketing, rooms/food and beverage operation, accounting and renovation. Our team has had extensive experience with most major franchises, which recognize Driftwood for its commitment to excellence. In addition to those brands named above, the company is an approved operator for Westin, Omni, Ramada, Embassy Suites, Doubletree Club and several others.

Since its inception in 1999, Driftwood has consistently achieved exceptional growth. We have assembled an experienced and entrepreneurial management team capable of achieving focused objectives. Members of the company's senior management have an average of 20 years of experience in all segments of the lodging industry, and have proved highly successful in the takeover, re-positioning, and optimization of hotel operations.

Driftwood Hospitality Management, LLC is located in Jupiter, Florida, with additional offices in Miami, Florida; San Jose, Costa Rica and Scottsdale, Arizona.

Meet the Management Team Behind the Winning Strategy

At Driftwood, we are proud of our success in achieving strong revenue generation and solid growth in Net Operating Income at our portfolio hotels and resorts. We are well-positioned to continue our growth in to the future. We are confident that our company will be able to capitalize on its experience and expertise in acquiring, developing, repositioning, renovating and operating hotels by selecting unique opportunities in attractive markets.

Significant company highlights include:

- Growth to the current size of 44 hotels and resorts encompassing over 8,900 rooms throughout North America and Costa Rica.
  Driftwood combined total revenues exceed $250,000,000
- Over 30 corporate employees focusing on hotel operations, sales and marketing, Internet strategy and online distribution, development acquisitions, renovation, accounting, and yield management.
- Investment in Grupo Vacacional Cardel, Ltd., an innovative Vacation Club ownership programme with marketing offices throughout Latin America. The programme enables Driftwood managed properties to boost hotel occupancies during traditionally slow periods. GVC is affiliated with the RCI worldwide exchange network.

Management Services

Turning Problems into Solutions and Challenges into Victories

Driftwood Hospitality Management, LLC has assembled a very experienced and entrepreneurial management team that is capable of completing its operating strategy. The members of the company's senior management have an average of 20 years of experience in all segments of the lodging industry.

The company provides centralized corporate support services in accounting, payroll, data processing, financial analysis and risk management; interior design and renovation; sales, marketing, Internet distribution, eMarketing and advertising; human resources management, and vendor purchases. At the same time, we encourage entrepreneurial spirit and empower hotel associates to take initiative and actively contribute to their hotel's success.

Driftwood Hospitality has adopted a comprehensive strategy to become the most Internet-savvy hotel management company in the world. Our top priorities include the expansion of our hotels' Internet presence, a continual increase in online bookings, especially from the direct online channel, and the development of an individualized eMarketing and eDistribution plan for everyone of our properties.

Investment

Growing Investments with a Proven Track Record

Driftwood Hospitality Management establishes venture partnerships with outside equity investors. Each investment partnership owns the hotel to be acquired. The investing equity sponsor will receive priority returns and shares of hotel profits from operations or sales. The company manages the ventures and hotels for a market rate fee and will share in the profits from operation and sales.

Since January 1994, key members of the Driftwood Hospitality management team have successfully completed the acquisition and development of 90 hotels. Driftwood has extensive operating experience with the major hotel franchises, including Hilton, Radisson, Sheraton, Crowne Plaza, Wyndham, Westin, Omni, Holiday Inn, Ramada and others.

Due to our strong fee base and strength of our balance sheet, we are able to provide extensive service and coverage to all assets in our portfolio. We are well-positioned to assume the management of additional properties in the near future. This is a significant benefit to new clients of the company, because we can initiate a takeover of a new hotel in an expedient manner and provide corporate oversight from seasoned hotel executives, ensuring that guest satisfaction and financial returns at the new hotel are maximized immediately.

Acquisition and Development

Creating Exceptional Asset Value

Since January 1994, the Driftwood Hospitality management team has successfully completed the acquisition and development of 90 hotels.

The company believes it has access to opportunities which may not be identified or available to others, due to the following key attributes:

- Significant experience of the company's management team.
- Employment of robust Internet distribution and e-Marketing strategy.
- In-depth knowledge of local markets and destinations.
- Size and geographic diversity of past portfolio hotels.
- Personal relationships with numerous hotel owners, tour operators, meeting planners and wholesalers.

Information regarding potential opportunities originates within the Company as well as through outside sources. Further, our established track record of generating significant operating profits from our portfolio hotels creates invaluable credibility when approaching potential partners and financial resources within the hospitality industry.

Repositioning and Renovations

Driftwood is actively engaged in initiating and overseeing renovations of under-performing properties. The company works toward repositioning these hotels based upon strategic plans designed to address the specific opportunities with each hotel's particular market. Renovations are chosen based on anticipated returns on investment, and include enhancing lobbies, restaurants, pools, beaches and guestrooms.

Hotel Operations

Our objective is simple: maximize services and minimize expenses. Driftwood Hospitality Management's experienced team offers the full complement of hotel and resort management services designed to maximize guest service and boost financial returns from day-to-day operations. The company's MIS systems monitor hotel level performance and ensure detailed reporting from each revenue and cost centre, focusing on such areas as room yields utilization, labour and cash management, expense variances and other items on a daily and weekly basis.

Productivity Management

Driftwood's team helps its portfolio hotels make the most of their manpower with specialized productivity management tools. By coordinating the property sales and service forecasts with its manpower needs, we target hours per occupied room, hours per cover and dollars per server to create the most efficient use of the hotel's most precious resource.

Food and Beverage Controls

Driftwood makes it possible for hotel food and beverage operations to be profitable again. In addition to the productivity management, the company also employs techniques to manage the property food and beverage costs. Our "food track" and "pour cost" programme help to maintain costs and minimize waste and pilferage. Programmes also assist hotel staff to design efficient yet trendy menus, control quality and maximize customer satisfaction.

Procurement

Driftwood's national and regional negotiated contracts guarantee that our managed hotels can obtain quality goods and services at the best possible prices.

Sales and Marketing

Driftwood Hospitality Management sales and marketing approach focuses on:

- Achieving optimum balance between Direct *vs.* Indirect Channel Sales.
- Taking full advantage of the Internet, online distribution channels and e-Marketing.

- Utilizing our in-depth knowledge of local market conditions.
- Working closely with group business generators, meeting planners, wholesalers, incentive travel companies, corporate travel departments, and franchise-sponsored marketing programmes.
- Deploying effective marketing campaigns.
- Employing effective sales incentive programme.
- Establishing professional sales administrative processes.
- Developing effective approaches to prospecting, qualifying, selling and closing.

Worldwide Sales Exposure

By working with major hotel brands and positioning our portfolio hotels on the Global Distribution Systems (GDS) and the Internet, Driftwood effectively provides global exposure to its hotels. Business and leisure travellers, meeting planners, travel agents and wholesalers from around the world can access and book the properties, giving Driftwood hotels unprecedented access to domestic and international markets.

Extensive European Exposure

Each Driftwood property benefits from a strong UK based marketing team. Our operations in Europe are highly regarded and afford each hotel and resort with high visibility and exposure to the customers and all European major tour operators.

Strategic Marketing Partnerships

Driftwood forms strategic partnerships with leading airlines, credit card and rent-a-car companies that enable our portfolio hotels to promote their products and services to consumers in innovative ways.

Customer Loyalty Programmes

By working closely with the major hotel brands and participating in their acclaimed loyalty programmes, Driftwood enables its portfolio hotels to offer a variety of perks to their customers, such as membership points, frequent flyer miles, upgrades and other value-added promotions.

Public Relations

Driftwood Hospitality employs robust public relations campaigns—both traditional offline and online—to help our portfolio hotels gain valuable exposure through the print and electronic media, in trade and consumer publications.

Co-op Advertising

Driftwood Hospitality is the producer and participant in co-op and joint advertising and promotional regional, national and international campaigns. This is a very effective and economical way to promote Driftwood properties in the print and electronic media.

Joint e-Mail Marketing Campaigns

Co-opetition is the right strategy in these difficult times. There has never been a better time for hospitality providers to work together with peers in the destinations we serve. Driftwood Hospitality is working closely with national tourist offices, local Convention and Visitors Bureaus and other partners to develop joint e-mail marketing campaigns focusing on its major destinations.

Media Purchasing

Driftwood Hospitality uses a centralized media buying approach to leverage the advertising dollars of its portfolio hotels. We work closely with our hotels to help create individual advertising campaigns. Through our media purchasing strategy, we assist properties in obtaining favourable industry rates for local advertising, enabling them to maximize their exposure and create exciting campaigns that really work.

Tradeshows and Showcases

Driftwood Hospitality sponsors participation in key industry tradeshows held all over the world. This participation ensures our hotels exposure to key decision-makers that can book their properties.

Internet Distribution Services

Internet Distribution and eMarketing

Driftwood Hospitality has undertaken aggressive efforts to maximize its properties' online performance. We have partnered with one of the leading e-Business consultants in the U.S., TIG Global, to support global and local Internet distribution strategies that will significantly enhance Internet revenues for every portfolio hotel. These strategies include website optimization, online booking technology, search engine strategy, destination web strategy, e-mail marketing, pay-per-click marketing, direct and indirect online distribution channel strategy.

Global Reservations Services

GDS Worldwide Reservations

Driftwood offers franchise and independent portfolio hotels instant global connectivity through the major Global Distribution Systems (GDS) and exposure to over 600,000 travel agents worldwide. We ensure that our properties are on all the major GDS systems, Sabre, Amadeus, Galileo/Apollo and Worldspan.

Interactive Reservations

Driftwood Hospitality portal websites and portfolio hotels' own websites employ state-of-the-art online reservation technology, allowing customers to make instant interactive bookings. Customers receive seamless connectivity and real time viewing of rates and availability with confirmed reservations within seconds.

Quality Control Services

Guest Feedback Programme

The best way to know how well our portfolio hotels are doing is to ask our guests. We provide a hotel evaluation tool that our properties can easily administer to each of their guests to measure performance and engage in continuous quality improvement. Our guest feedback programme provides immediate feedback so that our hotels can take immediate corrective actions. We also advise our hotels on steps to implement change.

Quality Control Services

Driftwood Hospitality takes a comprehensive look at the operation of the hotel from its guests' perspective. We follow the path of the guest from first encounter via phone or website through the entire guest experience. Our approach includes the specifics our hotels need to make meaningful customer service decisions. How long does it take for someone to pick up the phone at the front desk? Are staff name tags clearly stated? Are rooms kept tidy and drawn by a certain time of the day? These questions and many others are critical to meeting and maintaining the Driftwood Hospitality Management requirements. As a part of our service, we also evaluate cash handling, food ticket and beverage control and other critical auditing processes.

Safety Audit

Our loss prevention specialists are trained to evaluate a property from total loss prevention and assist in identifying "hot" spots on safety. We provide our portfolio hotels with complete training programmes for the hotel managers and line employees. In addition, we provide manuals and programmes for the ongoing maintenance of the property safety programme.

Manager on Duty Programme

We provide comprehensive, individualized "manager on duty programmes" including policy manuals, procedures and reports.

Employee Survey Programme

Positive employee morale translates into positive customer experiences. Our survey tool enables our portfolio hotels to determine employee moral. This objective survey determines areas of opportunity, weaknesses and strength among the property workforce. It enables the hotel general managers and executive staff to take constructive action to ensure maximum productivity and customer service.

Human Resource Management

Hiring Resources

Driftwood Hospitality utilizes sophisticated screening tools to enable properties to identify the best prospective associates.

Training Resources

Our training programmes are built on the tradition of providing customers with exceptional value and excellent service.

Payroll and Benefit Programmes

Our comprehensive programmes for franchised and independent properties improve operating efficiencies while reducing costs.

Revenue Management

Driftwood Hospitality analyzes market demand, historical trends, citywide and destination-wide trends and competitive pricing to predict and maximize revenue potential. We measure success by growing market share year-over-year and exceeding RevPAR goals. We are well-versed in the key processes for all major brands and optimize usage to maximize profit. Our processes and philosophy are both consistent and flexible to meet the needs of this dynamic aspect of our business.

The company's revenue management programmes focus on maximizing our properties' yield in rooms, food and beverage and ancillary revenue departments. We focus on programmes that help individual hotels maximize their real revenue opportunities in meaningful, goal-oriented ways.

Revenue Management Enhancement

Driftwood Hospitality works tirelessly to maximize RevPAR at its properties. Selling at the right price to the right customer at the right time is the norm at our portfolio hotels. In these tough times, we help every member of the property revenue management team to reach the right pricing mix in order to compete effectively and maximize potential revenues.

Revenue Management Training Programmes

Our comprehensive training programmes train hotel associates to look at revenues from a "demand/supply" perspective. We work with our Central Reservations operation to communicate the best rate and availability strategy on a daily basis. This programme includes computerized reports which compare results, forecast, budget and prior year histories. "RevMax" provides a simple, yet effective tool to manage daily, weekly and future revenue objectives.

HOTEL AND MOTEL MANAGEMENT

When talking with hoteliers all over the country, I find that one of the top challenges everyone faces is finding good, customer-focused associates and keeping them. Hopefully, you haven't gotten to the point where you say, "I just want them to be breathing!" Well, let's assume they are breathing and you have interviewed them for skills and behaviours you feel represent your company.

Get them in there and put them to work, right? Whoa! How hard did you have to work to find and select them? And if you followed the adage of "hire for personality, train for skills" let's make sure you start off on the right foot to keep them around.

It's basic customer service. We work very hard to treat our "external customers" well, to make them feel comfortable and welcome during their time with us. From pleasant curb appeal, to making sure our staff greets them instantly with a smile, it can't be any different with our "internal customers." We want both groups to be happy and return. Taking care of our internal customers is the first step to taking care of our external ones.

So, where do we start? Think back to your first day at work. How did you feel? Nervous? Excited? A little lost? As employers, these feelings need to be important to us. Turnover surveys indicate a major portion of employee departures happen in their first 90 days. Why is that? What are we doing (or not doing) that causes someone who wanted to join our team to change their mind?

We have a window of opportunity to take an employee's excitement about being on a new job and use it to build upon. Here are some things you can do to make these critically important people happier, more comfortable and open to our training. They may even stick around with the right attitude.

Day One

- Ask the employee to arrive at a time when someone has time to greet them.
- Make the team aware they are coming so everyone can welcome them. This makes both your new associate and the existing department members comfortable.
- Use bulletin boards or even marquees to say "Welcome Robert!"
- Give them a basic tour and introduce them to as many people as possible.

Within Week One

- Make sure they participate in an organized orientation. In a perfect world, this happens before they ever start their job and includes top management.
- Provide them with a partner/mentor during those first tenuous days.

- Have a skills training programme for them to participate in.
- Tailor training to the level of expertise they bring. Even experienced people need fine-tuning to your property's way of doing things.

Through the First 30 Days

- Get their feedback on the training they receive.
- Provide positive reinforcement on the things they do right.

At 90 Days

- Send them a card welcoming them as a "permanent member" of your team.
- Conduct a two-way performance review. Did you deliver a good foundation for their success?
- Review company benefits. Don't assume they remember what you said on day one.
- Make sure benefit paperwork is processed on a timely basis.

We need to consistently invest time to care for our service providers. Let these things tell them, "We are glad you are here. We're glad you're part of our team." It's also within this initial orientation period that you have the best opportunity to create "buy-in" to your corporate culture and standards of service. Ultimately, this investment will be more valuable to them than an extra $ .25 across the street.

Sales and Marketing

Driftwood Hospitality Management sales and marketing approach focuses on:

- Achieving optimum balance between Direct *vs.* Indirect Channel Sales.

- Taking full advantage of the Internet, online distribution channels and e-Marketing.
- Utilizing our in-depth knowledge of local market conditions.
- Working closely with group business generators, meeting planners, wholesalers, incentive travel companies, corporate travel departments, and franchise-sponsored marketing programmes.
- Deploying effective marketing campaigns.
- Employing effective sales incentive programme.
- Establishing professional sales administrative processes.
- Developing effective approaches to prospecting, qualifying, selling and closing.

Worldwide Sales Exposure

By working with major hotel brands and positioning our portfolio hotels on the Global Distribution Systems (GDS) and the Internet, Driftwood effectively provides global exposure to its hotels. Business and leisure travellers, meeting planners, travel agents and wholesalers from around the world can access and book the properties, giving Driftwood hotels unprecedented access to domestic and international markets.

Extensive European Exposure

Each Driftwood property benefits from a strong UK based marketing team. Our operations in Europe are highly regarded and afford each hotel and resort with high visibility and exposure to the customers and all European major tour operators.

Strategic Marketing Partnerships

Driftwood forms strategic partnerships with leading airlines, credit card and rent-a-car companies that enable our portfolio hotels to promote their products and services to consumers in innovative ways.

Customer Loyalty Programmes

By working closely with the major hotel brands and participating in their acclaimed loyalty programmes, Driftwood enables its portfolio hotels to offer a variety of perks to their customers, such as membership points, frequent flyer miles, upgrades and other value-added promotions.

Public Relations

Driftwood Hospitality employs robust public relations campaigns—both traditional offline and online—to help our portfolio hotels gain valuable exposure through the print and electronic media, in trade and consumer publications.

Co-op Advertising

Driftwood Hospitality is the producer and participant in co-op and joint advertising and promotional regional, national and international campaigns. This is a very effective and economical way to promote Driftwood properties in the print and electronic media.

Joint e-Mail Marketing Campaigns

Co-opetition is the right strategy in these difficult times. There has never been a better time for hospitality providers to work together with peers in the destinations we serve. Driftwood Hospitality is working closely with national tourist offices, local Convention and Visitors Bureaus and other partners to develop joint e-mail marketing campaigns focusing on its major destinations.

Media Purchasing

Driftwood Hospitality uses a centralized media buying approach to leverage the advertising dollars of its portfolio hotels. We work closely with our hotels to help create individual advertising campaigns. Through our media purchasing strategy, we assist properties in obtaining favourable industry rates for local advertising, enabling them to maximize their exposure and create exciting campaigns that really work.

Tradeshows and Showcases

Driftwood Hospitality sponsors participation in key industry tradeshows held all over the world. This participation ensures our hotels exposure to key decision-makers that can book their properties.

HOTEL MANAGEMENT TECHNOLOGY COURSE

Hotel and Restaurant Management Technology programme is designed to provide specialized occupational instruction in all phases of hotel and restaurant management. The programme prepares students for careers as managers/supervisors in the hospitality and tourism industry. Completion of the two-year programme leads to in Associate of Applied Science degree.

This programme targets the needs of entering students who want to develop skills required for entry jobs at the mid-management level in the hospitality industry and individuals already employed in the industry who need additional competence for possible advancement. Courses cover phases of food safety, sanitation, selection, production and handling, as well as, aspects of the common practices and management principles of the hospitality industry. Classes present a systematic approach to the flow of business through a hotel beginning with the reservation process and ending with the night audit. Texts include computer applications and use of the technology.

Additional emphasis is placed on nutrition and meeting the needs of customers, students, and clients in the hospitality industry, as well as, institutions such as nursing homes, schools and hospitals. Students work closely with area leaders in the industry through Delta Epsilon Chi, the Mississippi Restaurant Association, the Mississippi Hotel and Motel Association, the Dietary Managers Association, and the Convention and Visitors Bureau. Students who pass national certification exams receive certificates in designated areas which are recognized worldwide.

Enrollment is Open in Either the Fall or Spring Semesters

Entrance Requirement

Students enrolling in the Hotel and Restaurant Management Technology degree programme must present proof of a minimum ACT score of 10 in English and an overall composite score of 12 or have a TABE composite of 555 of higher.

Want more information? Use our Information Request form and submit it to us by E-mail. We can reply by U.S. Mail, E-mail or telephone.

NOTE: Graduates of this programme are required to score a 10.0 or better grade level on the Tests of Adult Basic Education—Level A (Reading, Math and Language). Academic assistance is available through the Related Studies Department.

HOTEL, MOTEL AND RESORT DESK CLERKS: US DEPT. OF LABOUR GUIDELINES

- Nature of the Work.
- Training, Other Qualifications and Advancement.
- Employment.
- Job Outlook.
- Projections Data.
- Earnings.
- OES Data.
- Related Occupations.
- Sources of Additional Information.

Significant Points

- Job opportunities should be good, because of industry growth and substantial replacement needs.

- Evening, weekend, and part-time work hours create the potential for flexible schedules.
- Professional appearance and personality are more important than formal academic training in getting a job.

Nature of the Work

Hotel, motel, and resort desk clerks are always in the public eye and are usually the first line of customer service for a lodging property. Their attitude and behaviour greatly influence the public's impressions of the establishment.

Front-desk clerks perform a variety of services for guests of hotels, motels, and other lodging establishments. Regardless of the type of accommodation, most desk clerks have similar responsibilities. They register arriving guests, assign rooms, and check out guests at the end of their stay. They also keep records of room assignments and other registration-related information on computers. When guests check out, desk clerks prepare and explain the charges and process payments.

Desk clerks answer questions about services, checkout times, the local community, or other matters of public interest. They report problems with guestrooms or public facilities to members of the house-keeping or maintenance staff. In larger hotels or in larger cities, desk clerks may refer queries about area attractions to a concierge and may direct more complicated questions to the appropriate manager.

In some smaller hotels and motels where smaller staffs are employed, clerks may take on a variety of additional responsibilities, such as bringing fresh linens to rooms, and they are often responsible for all front-office operations, information, and services. For example, they may perform the work of a book-keeper, advance reservation agent, cashier, laundry attendant, and telephone switchboard operator.

Work Environment

Hotels are open around the clock, creating the need for night and weekend work. About half of all desk clerks work a 40-hour week. Nearly one in five work part-time. Others work full-time, but with varying schedules. Most clerks work in areas that are clean, well lit, and relatively quiet, although lobbies can become crowded and noisy when busy. Many hotels have stringent dress guidelines for desk clerks.

Desk clerks may experience particularly hectic times during check-in and check-out times or when convention guests or large groups arrive at once. Moreover, dealing with irate guests can be stressful. Computer failures can further complicate an already busy time and add to stress levels. Hotel desk clerks may be on their feet most of the time and may occasionally be asked to lift heavy guest luggage.

Training, Other Qualifications, and Advancement

Employers look for clerks who are friendly and customer-service oriented, well groomed, and display maturity, self-confidence, and good judgement.

Education and Training

Most hotel, motel, and resort desk clerks receive orientation and training on the job. Orientation may include an explanation of the job duties and information about the establishment, such as the arrangement of guestrooms, availability of additional services, such as a business or fitness centre, and location of guest services, such as ice and vending machines, restaurants, and nearby retail stores and attractions. New employees learn job tasks under the guidance of a supervisor or an experienced desk clerk. They often receive additional training on interpersonal or customer service skills and on how to use the computerized reservation, room assignment, and billing systems and equipment. Desk clerks often learn new procedures and company policies after their initial training ends. While post-secondary education is not usually required for this job, formal training in a hospitality management degree or certificate programme may be an advantage for getting positions in larger or more upscale properties.

Other Qualifications

Desk clerks, especially in high-volume and higher-end properties, should be quick-thinking, energetic, and able to work as a member of a team. Hotel managers typically look for these personal characteristics when hiring desk clerks, because personality traits are difficult to teach. A clear speaking voice and fluency in English are essential when talking with guests and using the telephone or public-address systems. Good spelling and computer literacy are also needed because most of the work involves a computer. In addition, speaking a foreign language fluently is increasingly helpful because of the growing international clientele of many properties.

Advancement

Large hotel and motel chains may offer better opportunities for advancement than small, independently owned establishments. Large chains have more extensive career ladder programmes and may offer desk clerks an opportunity to participate in management training programmes. Also, the Educational Institute of the American Hotel and Lodging Association offers home-study or group-study courses in lodging management, which may help some desk clerks obtain promotions more rapidly.

Employment

Hotel, motel, and resort desk clerks held about 219,000 jobs in 2006. Almost all were in hotels, motels, and other establishments in the accommodation industry.

Job Outlook

Hotel, motel, and resort desk clerks will experience faster-than-average job growth through the 2006-16 decade because additional hotel properties continue to be built and more people are expected to travel for business and leisure. Good job opportunities are expected.

Employment Change

Employment of hotel, motel, and resort desk clerks is expected to grow 17 per cent between 2006 and 2016, which is faster than the average for all occupations. As more lodging establishments open and as people and companies have more money and travel more, occupancy rates will increase and create demand for desk clerks.

Employment of hotel and motel desk clerks should benefit from steady or increasing business and leisure travel. Shifts in preferences away from long vacations and toward long weekends and other, more frequent, shorter trips also should boost demand for these workers. While many lower budget and extended-stay establishments are being built to cater to families and the leisure traveller, many new luxury and resort accommodations also are opening to serve the upscale client. With the increased number of units requiring staff, employment opportunities for desk clerks should be good.

Growth of hotel, motel, and resort desk clerk jobs will be moderated somewhat by technology. Automated check-in and check-out procedures and on-line reservations networks free up staff time for other tasks and reduce the amount of time spent with each guest.

Job Prospects

In addition to job growth, job opportunities for hotel and motel desk clerks are expected to be good because of the need to replace the many clerks who either transfer to other occupations that offer better pay and advancement opportunities or who leave the workforce altogether. Opportunities for those willing to work a variable schedule should continue to be plentiful.

Projections Data

Projections Data from the National Employment Matrix						
Occupational title	*SOC Code*	*Employ-ment, 2006*	*Projected employment, 2016*	*Change, 2006-16*		*Detailed statistics*
				No.	*%*	

(Contd.)

Hotel, motel, and resort desk clerks	43-4081	219,000	257,000	38,000	17	PDF	zipped XLS

Note: Data in this table are rounded. See the discussion of the employment projections table in the Handbook introductory chapter on Occupational Information Included in the Handbook.

Employment of desk clerks is sensitive to cyclical swings in the economy. During recessions, vacation and business travel declines, and hotels and motels need fewer desk clerks. Similarly, employment is affected by special events, convention business, and seasonal fluctuations.

Earnings

Median annual earnings of hotel, motel and resort desk clerks were $18,460 in May 2006. The middle 50 per cent earned between $15,930 and $22,220. The lowest 10 per cent earned less than $13,690, and the highest 10 per cent earned more than $27,030.

Earnings of hotel, motel, and resort desk clerks vary by worker characteristics, season, and geographic factors, such as whether the establishment is in a major metropolitan area or a resort community. Earnings also vary according to the size of the hotel and the level of service offered. For example, luxury hotels that offer guests more personal attention and a greater number of services typically have stricter and more demanding requirements for their desk staff and often provide higher earnings.

Related Occupations

Lodging managers, particularly at smaller hotels and lodging establishments, may perform some of the same duties as desk clerks. Other occupations that require workers to assist the public include counter and rental clerks, customer service representatives, receptionists and information clerks, and retail salespersons.

OOH ONET Codes

Suggested citation: Bureau of Labour Statistics, U.S. Department of Labour, *Occupational Outlook Handbook, 2008-09 Edition,* Hotel, Motel, and Resort Desk Clerks, on the Internet at http://www.bls.gov/oco/ocos132.htm.

Resort Data Processing Inc.

Resort Data Processing, Inc. (RDP) is a property management software company founded in 1981 and headquartered in Vail, Colorado. RDP develops, installs, and provides 24-hour support for Vacation Rentals, Condominium-Hotels, Resorts, Hotels, Campgrounds, and Timeshare/Fractional ownership/club membership systems with over 1,000 installations worldwide.

Why Resort Data Processing?

- Over 25 years in the business.
- Support 24/hours day, 365 days a year.
- RDP helps generate more revenue.
- Our software adapts to the needs of the customer, not vice-versa.
- RDP provides personal service and direct contact with management.
- We will add custom features.
- RDP provides an unprecedented level of control of the configuration of the system and presentation of your data. Our philosophy is to allow customers to easily change reports, screens, confirmations, folios, statements and more, without calling RDP support.

Vacation Rentals, Condo-Hotels, Timeshare

Use the links below to learn about RDP solutions for Vacation Rentals, Condo-Hotels, and Timeshare Resorts designed to maximize owner satisfaction and increase management revenue.

Hotels, Resorts, Campgrounds

Use the links below for more information regarding Resort Data Processing's complete Windows based solution for Hotels & Resorts. Over 1000 installations since 1981 with 24 hours/365 day support.

Hardware and Technology

Use the links below to learn about RDP technology, including hardware requirements, Interfaces, crystal reports, sample screens, e-mail marketing and more.

Why Buy from Resort Data Processing?

A message from barry Biegler, President and Founder, Resort Data Processing, Inc.

Why should you buy property management software from Resort Data Processing? This website is filled with many potential reasons, but here are five of the most important:

1. RDP helps you generate significantly more revenue.
2. Our software adapts to the needs of the customer; not vice-versa.
3. We provide an unprecedented level of control of the configuration of the system and presentation of your data. Our philosophy is to allow customers to easily change reports, screens, confirmations, folios, statements and more, without calling RDP.
4. We are a small company which provides personal service and direct contact with top management to get things done quickly.
5. RDP has been in business over 25 years. We know what we're doing. We are a very solid company financially, so we will be here in the future to support and improve the system.

Each of these points is explained in more detail below:

- Vacation rentals and condominium hotels.
- Hotels and resorts.
- Timeshare and club membership.
- Campgrounds.
- Internet reservations.
- Travel services.
- Technology overview—RDPWin.
- Hardware requirements.
- Resort data processing company overview.
- Customer list.
- RDP partners.
- Available interfaces (POS, Phone, GDS, etc.).
- Support home page.
- Pricing and proposals.
- Samples screens.
- Home page-–www.resortdata.com.
- Recent news and events.
- Pictures of RDP headquarters.
- Site map for ResortData.com.

Generate Customer Profits

Most property management software companies talk about cutting expenses via "ease-of-use" or saving employee time. While we believe cutting expenses is important, and our software can help in this area, we would rather focus our efforts on generating significant additional income for our customers. Some of the revenue generating tools that are part of RDP are:

- Integrated yield management with detailed documentation on how to implement it. Our average customer has increased revenue by over $200,000/year.
- Our Internet Reservation Module allows guests to make reservations over the Internet 24 hours a day, 365 days a year, directly into the RDP system without paying reservation commissions. We also provide extensive

training on how to make your website more "findable" on the Internet.

- We have various marketing tools (such as integrated e-mail to guests, groups, travel agents, wholesalers, etc.).
- Our RDPConnect programme provides low-cost connectivity to the Global Distribution System (GDS), so your property receives its share of reservations from travel agents and thousands of websites such as www.Travelocity.com. We also provide no-cost consulting on how to maximize your GDS exposure and revenue.
- Our annual customer conference in Vail, Colorado, brings together hundreds of companies similar to yours. While providing in-depth training, the focus of the conference is to brainstorm with our customers to determine what else we can do to help them make money. Most of RDP's best features have come from customers.
- Our research and development, documentation, and training are all focused on increasing customer profit. Our competition often worries about implementing new technology just because it's new. At RDP, we focus on only implementing whatever technology we need to help you make money. And our track record shows we have been very good at it over the years. Take a moment to review our Windows-based software RDPWin.

RDP Adapts to the Customer

RDP believes software should adapt to the needs of the individual customer instead of forcing the customer to adapt to the software. While this seems like a self-evident truth, you may find that many of our competitors believe otherwise and have a "take it or leave it attitude." (*i.e.*, you either use the software the way it is, or you don't use it at all).

Your business is very important to us. If this means we have to change our software to make close the deal, then we will. More than half of our 1000 customers have a unique feature was added just for them. To avoid confusion, we add these features with switches so that the feature is only active for specific customers.

Our software is designed so you can configure it to operate the way your business works. If you can't, we will change it so you can.

Control Your System and Data Analysis, Export/Import and More

RDP provides an unprecedented level of system configuration control and presentation of your data. Our philosophy is to allow customers to easily change reports, screens, confirmations, folios, statements, and more (without calling RDP).

- Over 400 system reports using Crystal can be printed, e-mailed, or exported to Excel, Adobe, and other formats.
- Reservation Analysis screens are available for reservation detail, transactions, and more.
- Data is located on a file server under your control for high performance and security.
- Guest confirmations, folios, and marketing materials can include your logo and pictures, and you can easily change them at any time.
- Accounting data can be exported to third party systems.
- Mass e-mails can easily be created for guests, owners, travel agents, groups, and more with images, newsletters, etc.
- For Vacation Rental and Condo-Hotels, owners can use the Internet to view owner statements, make reservations, enter work orders, and much more.

Customers Stay in Direct Contact with Top Management

While RDP has been in business for more than 25 years, we have not allowed the company to grow into a bureaucratic nightmare. We are still a small company with direct contact between top management and customers.

We have become friends with our customers over the years. Our annual customer conference in Vail, Colorado, has the feeling of a family gathering: not a corporate function. This is a very important element of who we are, as it is always much more fun to help a friend with a problem than a customer.

My name is Barry Biegler, and I'm the President and Founder of Resort Data Processing, Inc. My direct, personal phone number is 970-845-1157. I believe my #1 job is to talk to customers and prospects to help answer questions.

With most companies, it is almost impossible to find someone who is in charge and actually able to make a decision. There are legions of people who screen calls and redirect customers. At RDP, everyone answers their own phone. If you ever have a problem with my company or need something, just give me a call.

Company Stability—Over 25 Years and Solid Financial Position

If the company you purchase software from goes out of business, the software becomes effectively worthless. This is because the software is only 15 per cent of the solution. The other 85 per cent is technical support, product updates, onsite training, etc. RDP has been in business over 25 years. We are very solid financially, with no company debt. We have sold over 1,000 systems, which provides an installed base of support contracts to insure we will be in business for many years to come.

Summary—Why Buy From RDP

When you purchase a Property Management System (PMS), we believe it is more important to look at the character of the company who creates the software than the technical system details.

All of the major PMS vendors handle the basics: reservations, check-in, check-out, audit, etc. The key to a PMS purchase is to understand that the software is only the beginning of a partnership between two companies. Many of our competitors believe it's all about the software. Nothing could be farther from the truth. It's all about the people.

A software vendor can tell you anything in a brochure or in a demo; so please check our story with our customers. Ask them if our support people actually answer the phone immediately. Find out if our Yield Management and Internet Reservation Module are making them money. Ask our customers if the system is flexible enough for them and adapts to their needs.

RDP truly is a different company. We have been in business for over 25 years with many of the same customers and employees. If you ever need anything from RDP, help is just a phone call away.

Hotel/Resort Software Overview

Resort Data Processing (RDP) software has been installed since 1981 at over 1000 locations worldwide (*see* customer list). Please use the links below to learn more about RDP software for Hotels and Resorts. If you are renting homes or condominiums on a short-term basis, please start with Vacation Rental Overview. Timeshare properties should begin with our Timeshare Resort Overview. Our Campground management system is also available. Our systems are fully integrated, so all features in our hotel system are available for vacation rentals and timeshare resorts and vice versa.

A printed brochure and pricing is available by calling 970-845-1140 or download the brochure in Microsoft Word or Adobe format.

Core RDP Modules	*Core RDP Modules*	*Interfaces*
• Technology Overview—RDPWIN • Sample Screens • Sample Reports • Reservations • Rates and Yield Management • Packages • Front Desk and Night Audit • Groups and Conferences	• Internet Reservation Module (IRM) • Vacation Rentals (Condo Accounting) • Timeshare and Interval Ownership • Campground Management • Guest Itinerary and Concierge • Activity Scheduling (bike rentals, etc.)	• Overview of All Interfaces • Global Distribution System (GDS) • Central Reservations • SDC Credit Card Interface • High Speed Credit Card Authorization • In-Room Video Check-out • Call Accounting

(Contd.)

Core RDP Modules	*Core RDP Modules*	*Interfaces*
• Travel Agents/Wholesalers • Guest History and Marketing • House-keeping Scheduling • General Ledger—Hotels • Trust Accounting—Owners • E-mail Marketing • Crystal Reports • Training • Hardware Requirements	• Wait List/ Denial Tracking/ Res Quotes • Frequent Guest/ Rewards • Work Orders and Asset Management • Booking Pace and Forecasting • Virtual Store on Internet • Messaging/To-do List • Change Tracking • 24-hour Support • Customer List • RDP Headquarters in Vail • Customer List and Comments	• Phone Actuator (On/Off) • Point of Sale • Voicemail • Maid-Phone (House-keeping) • Environmental • Back-office Accounting • Vacation Rental Trust Accounting • Nomadix Wireless Internet Billing • Room Key (Ving Card, etc.) • RDP Partners and Alliances

Vacation Rental and Condo-Hotel Features and Links

Maximizing owner satisfaction and increasing management revenue since 1981

- Data Flows from Reservations to Owner Statement
- Full Trust Accounting Capabilities
- Equalize Owner Rental Revenue
- Pay Bills for Owners and Guests
- Powerful Reservation Board (Tape Chart)
- Work Orders & Asset Management
- House-keeping Forecast, Schedule, and History
- Mix of Rental Types—Condos, Houses, Hotels, Timeshare
- Internet Reservations with Pictures and Virtual Tours
- Live Demonstration of Internet Reservations
- E-mail Integration for Guests, Owners, etc.
- Short-term and/or Long-term Rental
- Lock-off Units Allowed
- Various Billing Cycles—Monthly, Quarterly, etc.
- Split Revenue Across Billing Period
- Fast Production of Owner Statements
- Month-to-date and Year-to-date Totals Per Owner
- Statements Can Always be Reprinted
- Print Checks to Owners
- Integration to GDS, POS, Phones, Credit Cards, etc.
- Accounts Receivable with Aging
- Automatically Print or E-mail Overdue Notices
- IRS 1099 Year-End Reports
- Room Moves Pay Correct Owner
- Yield Management Integrated
- Sharewith Folios or One Guest With Multiple Folios

(Contd.)

- Manage Units not in the Rental Pool
- Extensive Custom Reporting with Crystal Reports
- Reservation Quotes, Wait List, and Denial Tracking
- Customer Relationship Management (CRM)
- Travel Agent Commissions Deducted
- Unlimited Charges per Owner
- Taxes Adjusted for Length of Stay and Location
- Timeshare and Interval Ownership Allowed
- All RDP Hotel Features Available for Owner Systems
- Customer List and Quotes
- Home Page—Vacation Rentals and Condominium Hotels
- Why Buy From RDP?

For Internet Reservation Demos see

- Vacation rental/condo-hotel.
- Timeshare IRM. net demo.
- Hotel/resort IRM.net demo.
- IRM.net for owner access.
- Sample IRM. net screens.
- Internet reservation overview.

Other Links in Resort Data.com

RDP Overview Topics

- Software overview.
- Why buy from RDP?
- RDP partners.
- RDPWin technology overview.
- Referral programme (*earn cash*).
- RDP customer list.
- New RDP modules.
- RDP corporate office.
- RDP news.

Internet Reservations (IRM)

- Internet reservations overview.
- Condominium IRM demo.
- Hotel IRM demo.
- IRM customer sites.

- IRM customer quotes.
- New features.
- IRM hardware requirements.
- E-mail marketing.

General

- Support home page.
- Training.
- Global distribution system.
- New preprinted forms.
- RDP partners and alliances.
- Hardware requirements.
- High-speed credit card processing.
- RDP interfaces available.

Vacation Rental and Condo-Hotel Overview

RDP was founded in 1981 to develop software for Vacation Rentals and Condo-Hotels. We now have over 1000 customers and 26 years experience with the complex world of reservations and owner trust accounting. This section describes our Vacation Rental and Condo-Hotel features, designed for managing individually owned homes or condominiums that are rented on a short term and/or long term basis (daily, weekly, monthly or yearly). Please see our Product overview page information on our products for hotels, timeshare, and campgrounds. Maximizing owner satisfaction and increasing management revenue since 1981.

- Reservations,
- Internet reservations,
- GDS reservations,
- E-mail confirmations,
- Integrated E-mail,
- Reservation tape chart,
- Yield management,
- Guest itinerary,

- Packages,
- Travel agents,
- Groups and conferences,
- Guest history,
- Long-term rentals,
- Change tracking,
- Denial tracking work orders,
- Owner internet access,
- Unique rates per owner,
- Pay bills for owners,
- Owner year-to-date totals,
- Split owner revenue across months,
- Owner receivables,
- 1099 and 1042S Reports,
- Bill house-keeping to owners,
- Owner statements on-line,
- Trust accounting,
- Equalize owner revenue,
- Lock-offs supported,
- Vacation Insurance and services sample screens,
- Hardware requirements,
- Manage non-rental units,
- Customize reports,
- Interfaces,
- PCI compliant credit cards,
- High speed credit card authorization,
- On-site installation,
- 24-hours support,
- RDP replaces First resorts, and
- RDP Partners and Alliances.

Sample Owner Statement

A wide variety of data flows automatically into the owner statement, as represented by the diagram below. Features include:

- Statement cycles can be monthly, quarterly, or other.
- All data automatically flows from work orders, housekeeping, and reservations to the statements.
- Owner statements can be printed and mailed or e-mailed as an Adobe PDF file.
- Checks can be printed and mailed.
- Owners can use the Internet to view or print current and past statements with proper password.
- Owners can make reservations and check their calendar via the Internet.

Owner Statement—Monthly

Owner Statement—MTD/YTD Recap

Data Flow from Reservations, Work Orders, and House-keeping to Owner Statement and General Ledger/Trust Accounting

Information flows automatically from Reservations, Work Orders and House-keeping to the Owner Statement and Trust Accounting system as follows:

Equalize Rental Revenue for Owners

RDP software helps equalize rental revenue for all owners and takes into account reservation length, seasons, property type, property location, owner use, guest of owner, and reservation cancellations. Various reports are available to show revenue per unit each month and year-to-date. Available units are displayed in "turn to be rented order" but still allow reservationists to select any available unit based on guest preferences to keep guests happy.

The RDP rental equalization logic is time tested, as it has now been in use for 26 years. Long standing RDP customers have analyzed the results and determined rental revenues fall within a few percentage points for similar units, while still allowing flexibility to select units based on guest preferences.

Additional Reservation Charges

Increase revenue beyond the management fee with additional reservation charges that are automatically calculated. These fees can be shared with the owner based on a unique percentage per owner or held 100 per cent by the management company. Examples of Additional Reservation charges include:

- Booking fees,
- Security deposits,
- Travel insurance,
- Cleaning fees,
- Cancellation charges,
- Gift items, and
- Guest activities (golf, skiing, boat rentals, etc.

Powerful Reservation Board (Tape Chart)

The system includes an online reservation board ("Tape Chart"). All new reservations, changes, and cancellations made using the internal RDP reservation system or by guests/owners using the Internet appear immediately on the Tape Chart. Dates, room numbers, and other reservation information can be changed graphically using the Tape Chart.

- Display reservations up to four years into the future.
- Filter by property and sort by room number, room type, or a customer-defined sequence.
- Filter using the guest preferences (shown above as #BR, LOC, PRC, etc.).
- Enter a number and click Find Room to quickly locate reservations in a particular room number.
- Reservations colors help distinguish by category for owners, maintenance, etc.
- Double-click a reservation tape or highlight a reservation and click the "Change Res" button to open the Change Reservation screen.

- Add reservations from the Tape Chart by just dragging the mouse over an empty date/room.
- Highlight a reservation and review the reservation details in the tabs below the grid (including the folio, work orders, house-keeping, etc.).
- The system tracks the market code and source of business for each reservation. Detailed statistical reports can then be printed to track marketing efforts. See *Sample Reports*.

Mix of Rental Types: Condos, Houses, Hotels, Timeshare

RDP can make reservations for a wide variety of rental units in the same system. For example, its possible to manage rental condominiums, non-rental units, hotel rooms, houses, timeshare units, campsites, and rental boats all in the same system. The reservationists simply make reservations for the various rental units, and the system tracks the owner payment on individually owned units. All features in RDP's hotel/resort system are available for use to our vacation/condo rental customers.

Owner and Guest Internet Access

RDP hosts a customer conference in Vail, Colorado to plan future research and development strategy based on customer feedback. In recent years, the focus has been to answer the question, "How can we use the Internet to make life easier and more profitable for our customers?" The answer is three-fold:

Guest Direct Internet Reservations (IRM)	Guests can book directly into the RDP system using our commission free Internet Reservation Module. See Internet Reservations Module.
Interface to Global Distribution System (GDS)	In addition to the commission free Internet Reservation Module, RDP offers an interface to the Global Distribution System (GDS) to load reservations from thousands of websites.
Owner Internet Access	RDP's capabilities for Owner Internet Access are explained below.

Owner Internet Access

The goal of RDP's owner Internet access is to identify all requests from owners that generate calls to management and move these functions to the Internet. Owner Internet access capabilities include:

- Secure, commission-free owner Internet access 24 hours/day, 365 days a year direct to your database.
- Owner and guest of owner Internet reservations.
- Owner calendar can be viewed, changed, and printed up to four years in the future.
- View or print all past owner statements on Internet in Adobe PDF format.
- Owners can review work orders for their units including complete detail.
- Owners can request house-keeping and specify requests using the Internet.
- Owner mass e-mail marketing and newsletters.
- Complete property descriptions with pictures.
- Commission free reservations using the Internet Reservation Module (IRM) for paying guests, groups, travel agents.
- Sell additional guest services (packages, golf, gift items etc.) with the Guest Itinerary and Concierge module.
- Additional reservation charges are allowed (booking fees, cleaning fees, etc.).
- All owner Internet access flows automatically to the Trust Accounting system.

Owner Internet Access Capabilities

A few sample screens from the Internet reservation module appear below. For additional information, please use the following links:

- Internet reservation module overview.
- E-mail marketing.

- Owner accounting.

E-mail Integration for Guests, Owners, Travel Agents, etc.

E-mail is one of the most powerful and least expensive marketing tools available and has been fully incorporated into the RDP system at no additional charge. E-mail features included:

- Automatically send guest confirmations using RDPWin E-mail monitor in adobe and other formats.
- E-mail owner statements. Owners can also print statements directly from the Internet.
- E-mail marketing databases are created for guests, travel agents, groups, wholesalers, and condo/timeshare owners.
- Mass e-mails can be sent directly from the RDP system with no third-party software required.
- Reservationists can easily e-mail guests pictures of the property, directions, maps, and other attachments.
- RDP abides by all current regulations for anti-SPAM by allowing guests to "opt out" of mass e-mails.
- Crystal Reports can be created and distributed by e-mail.
- Reservations made by the Internet Reservation Module (IRM) generate and send e-mail confirmations.
- Owner newsletters can be automatically sent via e-mail.

Overview of E-mail Marketing for additional information

E-mails can be sent to all owners in a matter of minutes with either a hand-typed message or an attachment (such as a Word or Adobe document).

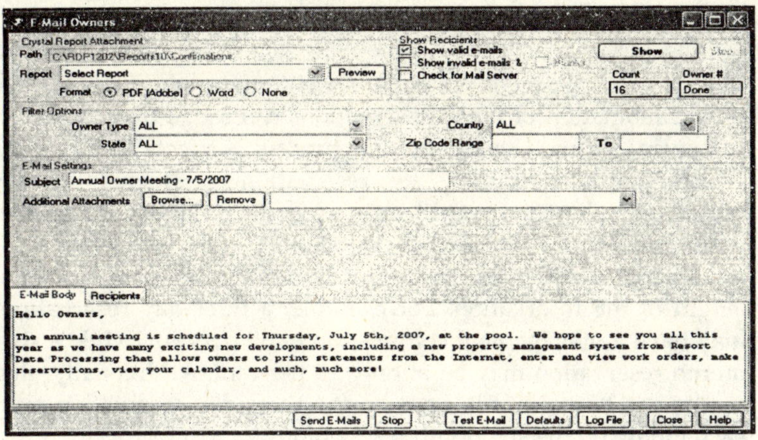
E-Mail Owners
Crystal Report Attachment
Path
Report Select Report
Preview
Format PDF (Adobe) Word None
Show Recipients
Show valid e-mails
Show invalid e-mails &
Check for Mail Server
Show
Count 16
Owner # Done
Filter Options
Owner Type ALL
State ALL
Country ALL
Zip Code Range
To
E-Mail Settings
Subject Annual Owner Meeting - 7/5/2007
Additional Attachments
Browse...
Remove
E-Mail Body
Recipients
Hello Owners,
The annual meeting is scheduled for Thursday, July 5th, 2007, at the pool. We hope to see you all this year as we have amny exciting new developments, including a new property management system from Resort Data Processing that allows owners to print statements from the Internet, enter and view work orders, make reservations, view your calendar, and much, much more!
Send E-Mails
Stop
Test E-Mail
Defaults
Log File
Close
Help

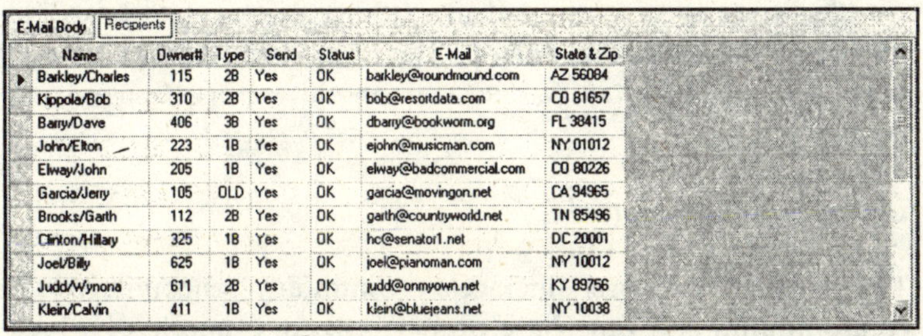
E-Mail Body
Recipients
Name Owner# Type Send Status E-Mail State & Zip
Barkley/Charles 115 2B Yes OK barkley@roundmound.com AZ 56084
Kippola/Bob 310 2B Yes OK bob@resortdata.com CO 81657
Barry/Dave 406 3B Yes OK dbarry@bookworm.org FL 38415
John/Elton 223 1B Yes OK ejohn@musicman.com NY 01012
Elway/John 205 1B Yes OK elway@badcommercial.com CO 80226
Garcia/Jerry 105 OLD Yes OK garcia@movingon.net CA 94965
Brooks/Garth 112 2B Yes OK garth@countryworld.net TN 85496
Clinton/Hillary 325 1B Yes OK hc@senator1.net DC 20001
Joel/Billy 625 1B Yes OK joel@pianoman.com NY 10012
Judd/Wynona 611 2B Yes OK judd@onmyown.net KY 89756
Klein/Calvin 411 1B Yes OK klein@bluejeans.net NY 10038

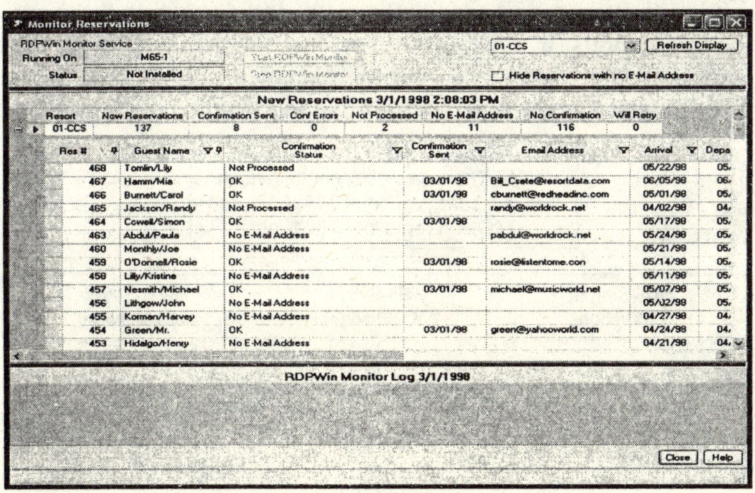
Monitor Reservations
RDPWin Monitor Service
Running On M65-1
Status Not Installed
01-CCS
Refresh Display
Hide Reservations with no E-Mail Address
New Reservations 3/1/1998 2:08:03 PM
Resort New Reservations Confirmation Sent Conf Errors Not Processed No E-Mail Address No Confirmation Will Retry
01-CCS 137 8 0 2 11 116 0
Res # Guest Name Confirmation Status Confirmation Sent Email Address Arrival Depa
468 Tomlin/Lily Not Processed 05/22/98
467 Hamm/Mia OK 03/01/98 Bill_Csete@resortdata.com 06/05/98
466 Burnett/Carol OK 03/01/98 cburnett@redheadinc.com 05/01/98
465 Jackson/Randy Not Processed randy@worldrock.net 04/02/98
464 Cowell/Simon OK 03/01/98 05/17/98
463 Abdul/Paula No E-Mail Address pabdul@worldrock.net 05/24/98
460 Monthly/Joe No E-Mail Address 05/21/98
459 O'Donnell/Rosie OK 03/01/98 rosie@listentome.con 05/14/98
458 Lilly/Kristine No E-Mail Address 05/11/98
457 Nesmith/Michael OK 03/01/98 michael@musicworld.net 05/07/98
456 Lithgow/John No E-Mail Address 05/02/98
455 Korman/Harvey No E-Mail Address 04/27/98
454 Green/Mr. OK 03/01/98 green@yahooworld.com 04/24/98
453 Hidalgo/Henry No E-Mail Address 04/21/98
RDPWin Monitor Log 3/1/1998
Close
Help

Short and Long-term Rental

The system is designed for either short-term or long-term rentals or a combination of both. Reservations can range from one-day to several years. The reservation process is identical for both, which simplifies training for reservationists. Rooms can be rented both short-term and long-term or even removed from the rental programme for selected periods.

Charge a different management commission based on the length of the reservation. For example, a three-day reservation may have a management commission of 35 per cent, while a six-month reservation may be at only 10 per cent. Additionally, the owner can be paid only once on the three-day reservation and each month on the six-month reservation.

The system can automatically adjust the tax rate based on the length of stay. For example, a three-day reservation may have a 9 per cent tax, while a six-month reservation is non-taxable.

Lock-off Units Supported

The system supports lock-offs (commonly encountered at condominium and timeshare properties). An example of a lock-off is a three bedroom unit that can be rented as either three one-bedroom units, a two-bedroom and a one-bedroom unit, or a three-bedroom unit. The system calculates rates based on the configuration of the unit. An example follows:

34M—The three room condominium that is a combination of 34A, 34B, and 34C and rents for $280/Night

34A-Single, $100/Night	34B-Single, $100/Night	34C-Single, $100/Night

34D—A two bedroom combination of 34A and 34B and rents for $185/Night

Non-rental House or Condominium Management (Owners not in Rental Pool)

Many of RDP's customers use the system to manage homes or condominiums that are not in the rental pool. Features include:

- Easily place a unit into or remove from the rental pool.
- Include a unit in the rental pool for only part of the year.
- Owners of non-rental units can still use the Internet Reservation Module to indicate use for themselves or guests.
- RDP's Work Orders and Asset Management Module can be used to schedule and track all maintenance of rental or non-rental units as well as any assets in the units themselves.

Extensive Custom Reporting Available with Crystal Reports

RDP software includes much more report writing capability than First Resorts. RDP uses Crystal Reports as the basis for over 300 Reports. During installation, RDP modifies those reports and creates new ones to meet the unique requirements of each customer. After installation, customers can create custom reports or modify system reports using Crystal Reports Version 10 Standard Edition. Crystal Reports is a full Windows product and allows the use of graphics, colors, charts, and fonts that improve the look of all guest correspondence.

Please use the following links for more information:

- Crystal reports overview.
- Sample reports.
- RDP owner accounting overview.

Work Orders and Asset Management

Key concepts of the Work Orders and Asset Management module include:

- Employees can enter work orders from any workstation at the property (front desk, maintenance office, etc.).
- Owners can view work orders over the Internet.
- New work orders appear immediately on the monitor in the maintenance department.
- Employees or third party vendors can be assigned to the work order.
- An e-mail can be automatically sent to the cell phone of the person assigned to the work order.
- All time and materials used on the work order can be tracked.
- Checks can be generated to work order vendors and owners billed (all from one screen).
- All property assets can be entered (pool heater, desk, television, etc.).
- Contents of each owner's unit can be tracked including model and serial numbers (refrigerator, dishwasher, etc.).
- Inventory tracking (supplies used to complete repairs).
- Work order history is maintained by vendor, owner and asset.
- All financial activity related to this module flows into trust accounting system.

Work Order and Asset Management Flow of Events

To illustrate the functions of the Work Orders and Asset Management module, consider the following example:

Guest Reports Problem	A guest discovers that the toilet is broken in the master bedroom and calls the management office. Any employee can enter the work order from any workstation using RDPWin and assign a priority (Low, High, etc.).
Assign Maintenance Person to Work Order	All new work orders immediately appear on the Work Order Monitor screen as a new work order with details such as "Fix the toilet in Room 101." The maintenance department can then assign the work order to a third-party vendor such as Bob's Plumbing or to an internal maintenance employee. Work Orders entered from workstations at the property can assign the work order when during the initial entry.

(*Contd.*)

Notification to Cell phone or E-mail	A text e-mail can be automatically sent to the cell phone of the maintenance employee. For outside vendors, an e-mail can be sent to request the work to be completed. The e-mail acts as a purchase order for services. E-mails to outside vendors are designed using Crystal Reports. See RDP E-mail Capabilities for more details.
Work Order Monitor Screen *Track Open Work Orders*	The Work Order Monitor then tracks the "open, assigned" work order. Any workstation can access the Work Order Monitor to track the progress of all work orders regardless of status based on level of access. Work order history is tracked for each outside vendor or maintenance employee. All work orders for any owner can be displayed. Repairs to specific assets are tracked such as all work to the pool heater.
Work Order Completed	When the assigned person completes the work order, change the status to closed and add any comments needed. The work order can track all time spent as well as all inventory items used (such as spending 45 minutes fixing the toilet; new toilet seal installed).
Pay Outside Vendor	Work orders can automatically pay a vendor. For example, call Bob's Plumbing to fix the toilet at a cost of $75, post the charge to the work order, and print a check to the vendor. A full statement is available for the vendor showing all repairs. All charges flow through the trust accounting system to provide a complete audit trail.
Bill the Guest, Group or Owner	The cost plus any mark-up of a work order can be charged to a guest, group, or owner. For example, pay Bob's Plumbing invoice of $75, but charge the charge the owner $95. The extra $20 represent management revenue.
Owner Statement	Charges for work orders appear on the owner statement with a full description of the work performed. See *sample owner statement.*
Asset Management	A complete history of all repairs for each "fixed asset" is available. Enter the "pool heater" as an asset including the serial number, description, which vendor to call for repair, and various other information. Each time a work order is generated for the pool heater, the vendor can be automatically notified by e-mail. The history of all repairs each asset is available.
Inventory	The system can maintain a list of inventory items. For example, you may have five toaster ovens in storage. When a toaster oven is removed from storage to replace one in a unit, inventory is tracked. When cost information is on the asset record, the owner or guest can be charged accordingly. A complete list of all inventory items is available.
Trust Accounting	All charges related to the work order (payments to vendors, charges to owners, inventory cost of items used, etc.) flow automatically to the Trust Accounting System.

(*Contd.*)

Batch Process Work Orders for Owners	In addition to billing owners individually for work orders, the system allows batch processing of all open work orders for all owners. The system can display all "work orders not charged to owners yet" to streamline billing owners for all unbilled work orders with just a few clicks.
Accounts Payable for Vendors	Vendors can be paid immediately for a completed work order with a check printed by the system. Alternatively, the system allows for accounts payables to be paid in batches, where numerous invoices from the same vendor can be paid periodically using only one check. All accounts payable information automatically feeds the Trust Accounting System.

- Work Orders and Asset Management
- Trust Accounting Overview

House-keeping Forecast, Schedule and History

The RDP system includes a very powerful house-keeping system which is designed to forecast house-keeping requirements, provide a daily cleaning schedule, and offers complete history by house-keeper and room.

Reservation Quotes, Wait List, and Denial Tracking

When a guest calls the reservation department at the property or your central reservations office, the reservationist has four choices:

1. File the reservation normally as a "real" reservation.
2. If the room is not available, the guest can be automatically added to the wait list for the dates and room type requested.
3. If the guest elects to not make the reservation, a "denied reservation" record is created to indicate why the guest did not complete the reservation.
4. The reservation can be saved as a "quote". For example, a guest may call and request prices on a room, along with scheduling three rounds of golf and a dinner. The guest may promise to "call back in a few minutes and book it". This reservation can be saved as a "quote". If the guest

calls back the reservationist can retrieve the "quoted reservation" and change it to a "real" reservation.

- Reservation quotes, wait list, and denial tracking.
- Reservation overview.
- Yield management.
- Internet reservations.
- Central reservations.

Customer Relationship Management (CRM) with Frequent Guest Programme

The Customer Relationship Management (CRM) module is designed to track all relationships with guests to improve guest service and marketing. All guest visits are tracked from one or more RDP systems. Points can be awarded for each reservation. The number of points can be different for different seasons, room types, total dollars spent, and other variables. Guests can make reservations by redeeming points. Restrictions can be applied to control when "point reservations" are allowed. A complete history is kept of all point reservations. Mass E-mails can be sent with attachments.

- Customer relationship management overview.
- RDP guest history system.
- E-mail marketing.

Travel Agent Commissions Deducted

The Travel Agent and Wholesalers system is completely integrated with the owner billing module. Travel agent commissions are automatically deducted from the owner statement. Various methods for calculating owner portions of the commission are allowed, including:

- Owner pays entire agent commission.
- Owner pays NO agent commission.

- Owner splits commission based on management fee. If the management receives 30 per cent of the rental income, the management also pays 30 per cent of the travel agent commission.
- Even split, 50 per cent each to management and owner, regardless of management commission.

Pay Bills for Owners and Guests

In addition to paying for work orders, it is possible to pay bills for owners and guests, such as cable TV, Electric, Gas, etc. The system can print checks to the vendors and bill either the owners on the owner statement or the guest on the reservation folio. The types of bills that can be paid for owners and reservations is as follows:

Type of Bill	*Explanation*
Work Order	A work order can pay the vendor who performed the works as well as generate a charge on the owner statement, including an optional mark-up. For example, if "Bob's TV Repair" fixes the owners TV for $100, you can pay the Vendor $100 and bill the owner $120, all from one screen. Checks can be printed for Vendors.
Recurring Monthly Charge	Accounts can be set up for recurring monthly charges that you pay on behalf of the owner. Examples include cable TV, electric bill, water bill, gas, etc. You can "batch process" the invoices each month from one screen. For example, if you receive 100 different electric bills for 100 owners, the system will display a screen of all 100 accounts and all you have to do is enter the amount for each account#. The system can then pay the electric company for all 100 invoices with one check AND charge each of the 100 owners.
One Time Payment for Owner	One time bills can also be paid for owners that are not related to a work order. For example, you may agree to pay an electric bill one time only for an owner.
Tasks for Reservations	It is also possible to have tasks on reservations, such as "purchase food and stock the refrigerator", and then charge the reservation and pay the Vendor.

Unlimited Charges Per Owner

The system automatically transfers gross reservation revenue and the management commission to the owner statement. In addition, transactions can be posted directly to the owner. The total of these charges is then deducted from the net reservation revenue. Charges can be posted to one owner at a time, or the system can automatically post the same charge to all owners. Charges can even be posted to all owners of the same unit type.

Various Billing Cycles—Monthly, Quarterly, etc.

Most management companies operate on a monthly owner billing cycle. However, the system can be used for any billing cycle. Owner statements can be printed once a week, once a month, every two months, once a quarter, etc. You can even mix billing cycles, so that one owner is paid once a week, another once a month, and a third only once a quarter.

Split Revenue Across Billing Periods

The system can split room revenue from the same reservation across two or more months. For example, if a reservation arrives 7/25/2008 and departs 8/6/2008, the owner could be paid July's portion in July and the remainder in August. Alternatively, all of the revenue can be paid to the owner in the month of checkout. Long-term rentals can pay the owner at the end of each month.

Month-to-Date and Year-to-Date Totals per Owner

The system produces a month-to-date and a year-to-date recap report per owner as part of the owner statement process. This report includes a total of room revenue, management commission, travel agent fees, credit card fees, and a sub-total for each direct expense category.

Statements can be Reprinted Forever

Owner statements can be reprinted for any past month or billing cycle: forever. For example, if an owner requests a copy of his statement from last March, it can be reprinted in seconds. Owner reservations, management commissions, travel agents fees, and all direct charges can also be instantly displayed for any time period.

Print Checks to Owners

The system can generate and print a check for the net amount due the owner each billing cycle. However, if the owner has more expenses than revenue, the system tracks this as an open receivable.

An owner's check may be held "on account" to offset future expenses. For example, one RDP customer has several owners who live in Mexico. These owners request that management hold their checks during the busy season to offset maintenance expenses during the slow season. These owners are marked as "generate checks = NO" during the busy season, preventing the system from automatically distributing a check each billing cycle.

Trust Accounting—Full General Ledger

One of the most important elements of Vacation Rentals and Condominium Hotels is Trust Accounting and General Ledger. The RDP system includes a full trust accounting system, which can be used as the only accounting system or in conjunction with another accounting system. Please see: Overview—RDP Trust Accounting for details.

Integration to GDS, POS, Credit Cards, Door Locks, Phone Mail, etc.

RDP interfaces with a wide variety of third party devices. Please use the links below for details.

Interfaces

- ❖ Overview of all interfaces.
- ❖ Global Distribution System (GDS).
- ❖ Central reservations.
- ❖ SDC credit card interface.
- ❖ High speed credit card authorization.
- ❖ In-room video checkout.
- ❖ Call accounting.
- ❖ Phone actuator (on/off).
- ❖ Point of sale.
- ❖ Voice-mail.
- ❖ Maid-Phone (House-keeping).
- ❖ Environmental.
- ❖ Back-office Accounting.
- ❖ Nomadix wireless internet billing.
- ❖ Room key (ving card, etc.).
- ❖ RDP partners and alliances.

Accounts Receivable with Aging

If the owner statement calculation produces a balance due to the management company, the system creates an owner accounts receivable (A/R). The A/R report is aged at 30, 60, 90 and 120 days. This report is available in a "one line per owner" format, or in a detail format showing each open item.

Print or E-mail Overdue Notices Automatically

If owners have not paid the amount due, the system can automatically post a late charge. Additionally, the system can print overdue notices, either on paper for mailing or sent to the owners via E-mail.

IRS 1099 and 1042S Reporting

The system automatically generates IRS 1099 reports at year-end. These reports show total revenue booked for each owner for the calendar year. Year-end reporting on magnetic media is required for larger properties and is available at no charge.

Room Moves Pay the Correct Owner

A room move can be performed using RDP's powerful online Tape Chart. For reservations moving between individually owned units, rental revenue for each owner is automatically calculated. For example, if a guest stays three nights in Room 101 and moves to Room 453 for two additional nights, RDP automatically pays Owner 101 for three days (minus management commission) and Owner 453 for two days.

Yield Management Integrated with New Reservations

RDP has integrated yield management with the reservation system. When combined with a careful study of the property's history and training of employees, yield management can significantly increases occupancy and average daily rate (ADR). Small increases in ADR can drastically increase property profit.

- Yield management overview.
- Hotel/ Resort Feature Overview (all features available to condo/vacation rental customers).

Sharewith Folios and one Guest with Multiple Folios

RDP supports both sharewith folios and one guest with multiple folios. A sharewith occurs when more than one guest is in the room and they wish to split the bill. For example, four guests could stay in a two-bedroom unit, with four different folios. Up to 99 sharewiths can split the charges for one room. One guest can also have multiple folios. For example, the room charges can go to Folio A and incidentals to Folio B. Room charges can be billed to the group master and incidentals for the guest. Please use the following links for more information:

- Front desk and night audit overview.
- Sample guest folio.

- Group/company billing overview.
- RDP owner accounting overview.

Taxes Adjusted for Length of Stay and Location

The system can automatically adjust the tax rate based on a variety of factors, including:

- *Length of stay*: For example, a three-day reservation may have a 9 per cent tax, while a six-month reservation is non-taxable.
- *Location of property*: If the room tax in Breckenridge is 8 per cent, while the adjoining town of Frisco is 7 per cent, and you rent houses or condominiums in both locations, the system automatically adjusts the tax.
- Non-taxable reservations, such as a church group.

Timeshare and Interval Ownership Allowed

The system can handle a wide variety of timeshare/ interval ownership concepts, including "point based", fixed week, floating week, quarter-share, eight-share, and a wide variety of other ownership situations. Combinations of these methods are possible, and it is possible to combine timeshare, whole ownership, and hotel rooms in one system. An example follows:

Timeshare/ Interval Ownership Topics

- Fixed week/floating/points and combinations.
- Timeshare owner access using internet.
- High capacity system with excellent performance.
- Invoice owners for dues and other charges.
- Auto-load owner reservations.
- Rental of owner time with automatic payment to Owners timeshare exchange reservations.
- Owner bonus time reservations.
- One owner statement for multiple weeks.

- ❖ Owner balance due interfaced to reservations.
- ❖ Track available weeks to sell.
- ❖ Owner dues and receivables.

All RDP Resort Features Available for Owner Systems

Please note that all features in our Hotel/Resort system are available for use with condominium, timeshare, and vacation rental systems.

HOTEL AND RESORT SOFTWARE: AN OVERVIEW

RDP was founded in 1981 to develop software for hotels and resorts. We now have over 1000 customers and 26 years experience with hotel management. This page describes our hotel and resort features. Please see our "Product overview" page for information on our software for Vacation Rentals, Condo-Hotels, Timeshare/Club Management and Campgrounds. RDP's Hotel & Resort software:

Core RDP Modules	*Additional Topics*	*Interfaces and Misc.*
• Reservations • Internet Reservation Module (IRM) • Central Reservations • Rates and Yield Management • Packages • Front Desk & Night Audit • Groups & Conferences • Travel Agents/Wholesalers • Guest History & Marketing • Guest Itinerary & Concierge • Conference Rm & Activity Scheduling • Guest Wait List • Denial Tracking	• Technology Overview—RDPWIN • Sample Screens • Sample Reports • Crystal Reports • Training • Hardware Requirements • Messaging/To-Do List • 24-Hour Support • About Resort Data Processing • RDP Headquarters in Vail • Customer List and Comments • Vacation Rentals/Condo-	• Overview of All Interfaces • Global Distribution System (GDS) • SDC Credit Card Interface • High Speed Credit Card • In-Room Video Checkout • Call Accounting • Phone Actuator (On/Off) • Point of Sale • Voicemail • Maid-Phone (Housekeeping) • Environmental • Back-office

(*Contd.*)

- Frequent Guest/Rewards
- House-keeping Scheduling
- General Ledger
- Reservation Change Tracking
- Work Orders & Asset Management
- E-mail Confirmations & Marketing
- Virtual Store on Internet

Hotels

- Timeshare & Interval Ownership
- Campground Management
- Vacation Rental Trust Accounting
- Preprinted Forms Available
- Vacation Insurance & Services

Accounting

- Nomadix Wireless Internet Billing
- Room Key (Ving Card, Kaba, etc.)
- RDP Partners and Alliances
- Referral Programme (Earn Cash)
- RDP Corporate Office

Sample RDP Property Management System Screens

Use the links below to view the sample RDP screens. Click on the header of any section for an overview, if available. A complete system overview is also available as well as sample reports.

Reservation Features	*Reservation Options*	*System*
• Configuration • Introduction • Find Reservation • New Reservations • Available Rooms • Yield Management • Analysis • Availability • Tape Chart • House Status • Unique Rates for Every Room • Held Deposits • Reservation Detail Tabs	• Change • Guest E-mail Confirmations • Add Room • Add Sharewith • Add Work Order • Guest Folio • Activities • Check In One or All • Check In Groups • Post Charges • Take Deposits/Payments • Issue Refund • Check Out One or All • Check Out Group Members • UnCheck-out • Cancel One Res • Cancel Groups • Uncancel Res	• RDPWin Log • Comment Labels • Add Rate Sets • Change Rate Sets' Defaults • Lowest Rate • Rate Plans • Rate Plan Patterns • DDF Info • Menu Security • RDPWin Monitor • System Configuration • SDC Configuration • VRS Configuration

Groups	*Agents*	*Owners*
• Introduction • Add • List • Find • Change • Adjust Room Blocks • Post Charges • Payments • Refunds • Statements	• Introduction • Add • List • Find • Change • Post Charges • Payments • Process Commissions • Statements	• Introduction • Add • List • Find • Change • Post Charges • Res Related Charges • Payments • Process Revenue • Reports • Statements • 1099 Electronic Filing • Audit Report

(Contd.)

Reporter (Crystal Reports)	*Stats*	*CRM*
• Reporter • Sample Reports	• Totals Room Revenue • Totals by Room Type • Totals by Room Type 2 BR	• Analysis • Configuration • Guest Information • Statements
Accounting	*House-keeping*	*Work Orders & Asset Management*
• Configuration • Add G/L Account • G/L Account List • Adjust Account Balances • Change Offset Accounts • Pay Taxes • Reconcile Bank Accounts • Check Vouchers • Trial Balance • Trust Summary • Trust Transfers	• Configuration • Schedule • History Analysis • History Analysis w/Prop. Code • History Display • History Change • Monitor Status • Room Status • Reports	• Introduction • Monitor—New • Monitor—Open • Monitor—Closed • Monitor—Closed & Grouped • Monitor—By Status & Vendor • Vendors • Vendors—Show Contacts • Vendors—Add Vendor • Vendors—Enter Invoice Amt • Vendors—Work Order Billing • Vendors—Statements • Resort Assets • Configuration

RDP Sample Reports

RDP provides over 300 standard reports, each of which can be customized with Crystal Reports. The reports listed below is a small sample of what is available. Additionally, you may click on the heading, such as Reservations, for an overview of that software. With Crystal Reports, you or RDP can create virtually any report required.

RDP offers a wide variety of pre-printed forms, such as folios or confirmations. *see* RDP forms or call 800-737-7277.

Sample Screens are also available for display, as well as a complete Software Overview.

These are just some of the reports available. With Crystal Reports, virtually any report can be created.

Reservations

- Individual Confirmation
- Group Confirmation
- Confirmation with Itinerary
- Reservations Made Today
- Reservations Canceled Today

Front Desk

- Arrival Report
- Departure Report
- Guest Folio
- Room Status—All Rooms
- House Status Report

Groups and Conferences

- Group Listing
- Group Statement
- Reservations by Group

Itinerary & Concierge

- Guest Tickets (Coupons)
- Activities by Vendor

Work Orders

- Work order Monitor & more

Night Audit

- Telephone Operator List
- Complete Transaction Report
- Payments by Method
- Advance Deposit Ledger
- Guest Ledger Balance Due
- Checked-Out Guests with Balance
- Daily Manager's Report
- Daily Manager's GL Recap
- Daily Flash Report
- Maintenance Rooms—Future
- Complimentary Reservations

Owner Accounting System

- Trust Accounting—Various Reports
- Vacation Rental System—Various
- Owner Statement
- Owner Statement w/ Shared Expenses
- MTD YTD Recap
- Owner 1099

House-keeping

- House-keeping Scheduling

Pre-Printed Forms Available

- See RDPForms

Call 800-737-7277

Stats/Analysis

- Market Code Analysis
- Monthly What-If Analysis
- Monthly Revenue Breakdown
- Rate Plan Comparison
- Revenue by Room Type
- Revenue by Source Code
- Revenue by State
- Revenue by Room Number
- Occupancy by Market Code
- Revenue by Market Code
- Revenue by Rate Plan
- Top 10 Travel Agents
- Top 10 States
- Top 10 Guests by Nights

Marketing

- Past Guest Marketing Letters
- Direct E-mail Marketing
- Guest Marketing (by Zip Code)

Forecasting

- 6 Month Forecast
- Comparisons to Previous Year

Appendices

APPENDIX I
WORLDWIDE LISTING OF ACCOUNTING/FINANCE/TAX RELATED WEBSITES

The Big Four

- Deloitte and Touche.
- Ernst and Young.
- PricewaterhouseCoopers.
- KPMG.

General

- Accounting Association of Australia and New Zealand (AAANZ).
- Accounting Net.
- Accounting.Org.
- Accounting Research Directory.
- Accounting Resources on the Internet (A Net).
- Accounting System Selection/Locator.
- American Institute of CPA's.
- Association of Chartered Certified Accountants (ACCA).
- Association of Certified Fraud Examiners.
- Audit Net.
- Australian Society of CPAs On-Line.
- AWT Allgemeine Wirschaftstreuhand—Horwath.
- British Accounting Association (BAA).
- British Association of Hospitality Accountants.
- CabinetLassa?d Dhaouadi.

- Canadian Association of Independent Accountants (CAIA).
- Canadian Institute of Chartered Accountants (CICA).
- Certified General Accountants (CGA) Association of Canada.
- Charter Group Partnership.
- Currency Exchange Rates.
- DFK International.
- e-FFE.co.uk (FF&E Budget Lists).
- Grand Thornton International.
- Grand Thornton (Vietnam) Ltd.
- Hansa Financials—Integrated Management Software for Hotels and Restaurants.
- Horwath.
- Hospitality Accounting Services.
- Hospitality Financial and Technology Professional.
- Institute of Certified Public Accountants of Singapore (ICPAS).
- Institute of Chartered Accountants in Australia (ICAA).
- Institute of Chartered Accountants in Ireland.
- Institute of Internal Auditors—UK.
- Internal Accounting Assoc. Auditor's Bookshelf.
- International Accounting Standards Committee (IASC).
- International Association for Financial Planning (IAFP).
- International Bureau of Fiscal Documentation.
- International Federation of Accountants (IFAC).
- International Group of Accounting Firms (IGAF).
- Nordic Accounting Network (NAN).
- Opimes—Revenue/Yield management.
- Ordre des comptables agrees du Quebec.
- Polaris International—An Association of Accounting Firms.
- PriceWaterhouseCoopers Thailand—Tax and Legal Services.
- Prologic First.
- Rutgers Accounting Web.

- Securities and Exchange Commission (SEC).
- Williams Denton Jones Accountants North Wales.

Publication Links

- Business Finance.
- Business Week Online.
- Computerworld.
- Datamation.
- Forbes.com.
- Fortune.
- Hotel and Motel Management.
- Hospitality Technology.
- Money.com.
- PC Computing Online.
- PC Week Online.
- The Wall Street Journal Interactive.

Tax, Tax, Tax

International Listings by Country

Argentina

- Administration Federal de Ingresos Publicos.
- Knowledge Net Country Profile.

Australia

Government Sites:

- Australian Government Home Page.
- Department of the Treasury.
- Review of Business Taxation—Treasury.
- New South Wales.
- Queensland.
- Victoria.
- Western Australia.

Other Resources

- Australian Professional Information Services.
- Australian Tax Practice.
- CCH Tax and Finance.
- Deloitte and Touche Taxing Times.
- Ernst and Young Taxation Gallery.
- ICAA Tax Reform Site.

Belarus

- Byelorussian Law.

Belgium

- Belgian Tax System.
- Index-Belgium Online.
- Ministry of Finance.
- SA Tax Advisers NV—Belgium Taxation.

Belize

- Belize Investment Guide.
- Ministry of Finance.

Brazil

- Ministry of Finance.

Canada

Government Sites:

- Department of Finance.
- Department of Justice.
- Government of Canada.
- Office of the Auditor General Provincial Tax.

- Alberta—Treasury.
- Manitoba—Department of Finance.
- New Brunswick—Department of Finance.
- New foundland and Labrador—Department of Finance.
- North west Territories—Department of Finance.
- Nova Scotia—Department of Finance.
- Ontario—Ministry of Finance.
- PrinceEdward Island—Provincial Treasury.
- Quebec—Ministere du Revenu.
- Saskatchewan—Department of Finance.
- Yukon Territory—Department of Finance.

Other Resources:

- Canadian Relocation and Expatriate Taxation Resource Centre.
- Canadian Tax Foundation.
- Canadian Tax Guide for Nonresidents.
- Canadian Tax Payers Federation.
- Cross Border Tax and Transactions.
- Deloitte and Touche Tax.
- Ernst and Young Tax Services.
- Quicken.ca- Tax Center.
- R&D Home Page.
- Tax Web.

Chile

- Servicio de Impuestos Internos.

Czech Republic

- Doing Business With Czech Republic.
- Knowledge Net Country Profile.
- The Chamber of Tax Consultants.

Denmark

- Ministry of Finance.

Estonia

- Estonian Investment Agency.
- Ministry of Finance.
- Ministry of Foreign Affairs.

Finland

- Finnish Tax Administration.
- Tullin Tietopalvelu (National Board of Customs).

France

- Club-Comptable.
- Ministerede l'Economie, des Finances et de l'Industrie-Republique Francaise.

Germany

- Internationales Steuerrecht.
- Steuerrechtim Internet.
- Steuer Thek:das Onlinenachschlagewerk fuer alle Steuerzahler.
- Tax Links.
- Texte derDeppelbesteuerungsabkommen (DBA).

Hong Kong

- Customsand Excise Department.
- General Tax Information.
- Inland Revenue Department.

Hungary

- Ministry of Finance.

India

- Ministry of Finance.
- Tax and you.

Ireland

- Chartered Accountants Taxation Summary.
- Institute of Taxation in Ireland.
- Revenue Commission.

Israel

- Ministry of Finance.

Italy

- Italian Fiscal System.
- Knowledge Net Country Profile.
- La Rosa and Associates.
- Minsterodelle Finanze.
- Taxline.

Japan

- Ministry of Finance.

Korea (South)

- Ministry of Finance and Economy.

Lithuania

- Ministry of Finance.

Luxembourg

- Ministry of Finance.

Malaysia

- Inland Revenue Department.
- Malaysian Association of CPAs.
- Malaysian Institute of Accountants.
- Treasury-Ministry of Finance.

Malta

- Customsand Excise Tax Act, 1997.
- Economy and Finance.
- Ministry of Finance and Commerce.
- White Paper on Taxation.

Mexico

- Secretariade Hacienda y Credito Publico.
- Serviciode Administracion Tributaria.

Moldova

- KPMG Tax Facts.

Monaco

- Monaco Taxation System.

Netherlands

- Belstingdienst.
- Fiscal up to date.
- Het Belastingparadies.
- Loyens and Volkmans—Tax Advisers.
- Ministry of Finance.
- Ministry of Finance—Taxation in the Netherlands.
- Ray's Links.

New Zealand

- CCH Tax Site.
- Inland Revenue Department.
- Knowledge Net Country Profile.
- New Zealand Treasury.

Norway

- Ministry of Finance and Customs.

Philippines

- Knowledge Net Country Profile.

Poland

- Poland Online—Tax System.

Portugal

- Impostos.net.

Russia

- Ernst and Young Russian Business Brief.
- Foreign Investment Promotion Centre.

- The ABC of Russian Business Law.

Saudi Arabia

- Business Tax.

Singapore

- Inland Revenue Authority of Singapore.
- Knowledge Net Country Profile.

Slovakia

- Ministry of Finance.

South Africa

- Butterworth Tax and Accounting Express.
- Department of Finance.
- Katz Commission Reports.
- South African Revenue Service (SARS).
- Value Added Tax.

Spain

- Asociacion Espanola de Asesores Fiscales.
- Knowledge Net Country Profile.
- Web Fiscal de Gesaf.
- Web Fiscal del Foro de Abogados Tributaristas.
- Web Fiscal IRPF.
- Web Fiscalpara Empresas.
- Web Gaceta Fiscal.

Sweden

- Finans Departememtet.
- KPMG Tax Facts.

- Riksskatteverket.
- National Tax Board.

Switzerland

- Department of Finance.
- Dr Tax Software.
- Institutfuer Steuerrecht.
- KPMG Tax Facts.
- OREF—Ordre Romand des Experts Fiscaux diplomes.
- Steuern.
- Taxation in Switzerland.

Taiwan

- Finance and Taxation.

Thailand

- Ministry of Finance.
- PriceWaterhouseCoopers Thailand—Tax and Legal Services.

Trinidad and Tobago

- Doing Business in Trinidad and Tobago—Taxation.

Tunisia

- Chambre Nationale des Conseils Fiscaux de Tunisie.

United Arab Emirates

- Ministry of Finance and Industry.

United Kingdom

Government Sites:

- CCTA Government Information Service.
- Customs and Excise.
- Inland Revenue.
- Parliament.
- Social Security.
- Treasury Department.

Other Resources:

- Accounting WEB Tax Facts.
- Accounting WEB Tax Zone.
- Chartered Institute of Taxation.
- Deloitte and Touche Tax.
- Ernst and Young Tax.
- Gray's Inn Chambers.
- Hazelwood Tax Facts.
- Institute of Fiscal Studies.
- PricewaterhouseCoopers Tax Centre.
- Pricewaerhouse Coopers UK Pocket Tax Guide.
- Ross Tax World.
- Thomson Tax On-Line.
- UK Taxation Directory.

Vietnam

- Grand Thornton (Vietnam) Ltd.

International Tax Sites

- Basic World Tax Code.
- Business Tax Info.
- Council of International Tax Education.

- Country Profiles.
- European-American Tax Institute.
- Foreign Earned Income Test.
- Inter-American Center of Tax Administration.
- International Association of Assessing Officers.
- International Spotlight.
- International Tax Software.
- International Tax and VAT Discussion Groups.
- International Tax Bulletins.
- International Tax Planning Association.
- International Tax Resources.
- International Tax Treaty Network.
- The Library.
- Global Tax Monitor.
- International Taxation Discussion Group Subscription.
- Revenue Canada.
- State Tax Links.
- Tax Forms (US).
- US Tax Code Online.
- US Treasury Department.

APPENDIX II
WORLD OF HOSPITALITY NET

WorldofHospitality.net aims to provide links to relevant information for event industry professionals, educators, students and researchers.

Within the Links Directory you will find a range of information, including careers, recruitment agencies, links to education programmes and a suppliers directory. For job vacancies and other career related resources, please visit the Careers/Employment section.

We have completely redesigned the site to improve the look and feel and to make it much easier to contribute links and other resources (including the ability to indicate country specific links/resources).

WorldofHospitality.net has also moved to a new hosting company to increase the speed and performance and allow a range of new features that will be introduced over the coming months.

(*i*) Hotel Software

miHotel Manager is a Windows® based Hospitality Software designed for hotels/motels. It is an extensive software package specially designed to help you manage your hotel. This type of application is sometimes referred as Property Management System in the hospitality industry. The many features includes: Hotel Guest Management, Hotel Reservation Management, Hotel Front Desk and Hotel accounting. User friendly interface, high speed and stability, client-server architecture, all these characteristics allows you to easily manage all the tasks for your hotel/motel. User Defined Fields for high flexibility, high-quality graphical representation of your rooms, real-time statistics... all these will help you to perform your duties faster, and with less effort.

(*ii*) Online Booking Manager

The <a href ="http://www.onlinebookingmanager.com"> Online Booking Manager</a> (http://www.onlinebooking-manager.com) is a unique multilingual system and a highly cost-effective method for promoting your accommodation services online. Hotels, motels, B&B, etc., who cannot afford large complex reservations systems can now successfully offer online bookings with the Online Booking Manager a low cost high performance solution for all hotels, motels, B&B owners.

(*iii*) Increase Bar Revenues

There are many ways for a bartender to increase revenues for his/her establishment and for him/herself. Get to know your regulars. Introduce yourself and ask them their names. If you have a hard time remembering names create a visual memory trick that will help you remember both their name and their favourite drink. I use very stark tricks connecting a name with the first letter of an animal and a visual of the animal with its drink. (*i.e.* Robert/Red Robin/Scarlet Ohara (Southern Comfort/ Cranberry Juice—R for the first name and animal/Red for the drink colour) When the customer enters ask them immediately if they would like their regular drink. They will enjoy that. Suggest some food that compliments the drink. If the drink isn't top shelf suggest a more expensive top shelf substitute. Once you are a little comfortable with the customer, suggest they bring a friend. With liquor and food prices commanding excellent margins you have just created some real revenues and profits. Once your regular customer brings a friend to the bar they will stay longer and eat and drink more. Your bar is livelier and more inviting to still more customers. On top of that you are enjoying yourself more while making more money!

APPENDIX III
INDIVIDUALIZED STUDIES IN INTERNATIONAL HOTEL MANAGEMENT

Individualized studies in international hotel management provides students with in-depth knowledge of international hospitality development and management. It focuses on international hotel operations with emphasis on U.S. corporate involvement in and planning for overseas expansions. It introduces students to the necessary management competency for global hotel management operations.

Objectives

- Understand the integration of tourism and the hospitality industry within national policies and plans.
- Analyze investment trends and hotel development patterns by international hospitality firms, and identify emerging overseas markets for hotel development.
- Understand the socio-economic impact of developing hotels in developing countries.
- Understand hotel management functions in a foreign country, such as human resources management, hotel marketing, financial control, accounting and taxes, and technology applications.
- Identify potential career development opportunities through internship programmes.

Required Courses

TSTD 220 International Hotel Management

Analysis of international hotel development and management functions with an emphasis on global manager competency. It encompasses political, economic, cultural, financial and legal aspects inherent in international business environment and their impacts on international hotel operations.

TSTD 278 Conference and Exposition Management

Site selection, programme planning and management, exhibits, selection and use of facility, volunteers, and budget management.

TSTD 290 Hotel Project Management

Examination of hotel project development, emphasis on market research, project planning, site selection, construction coordination, resource allocation, project scheduling, hotel valuation process, hotel marketing and pre-opening management.

FINA Real Estate Development

Examination of the forces that shape real state development; market analysis methods and techniques to evaluate project feasibility; the institutional and legal framework within which real estate development occurs and that influences controls, land value, and development potential.

APPENDIX IV
THE LODGING WIKI AT HOSPITALITY: A DETAILED LISTING

Hospitality-411

[96] Wine Country Inn and Gardens

Wine Country Inn and Gardens is a perfect choice for Napa Valley romantic getaways. The Inn began as one of the first Napa Valley Bed and Breakfast Inns and has transformed over the years to a stunning Boutique Hotel surrounded by rolling vineyards.

The Inn features luxury room, suite, and cottage accommodations with unbeatable amenities. Gull buffet breakfasts, in-room sound systems, restaurant shuttle, and afternoon wine and appetizers are all complimentary to guests. Excellent spa services are available as well as help with planning various day tours to surrounding wineries. Secluded pool and Jacuzzi as well as beautiful "secret gardens" are all within the grounds and waiting to be explored and enjoyed.

For a truly romantic Napa Valley vacation, the **Wine Country Inn and Gardens** is an excellent choice.

[90] Escape to Texas Hill Country

Texas Hill Country is a slice of heaven that encompasses more than 14,000 square miles of dude ranches, rivers, quaint towns, and rolling countryside. At the heart of Hill Country is the historic town of Fredericksburg. Named in Guideposts Magazine as one of the "Top 10 Small Towns in America", Fredericksburg is a popular destination for those escaping the urban sprawl of San Antonio and Austin. Church in Fredericksburt, TX and the surrounding Hill Country makes for a quaint and relaxing escape. Enjoy the nature and wildlife of the area, browse antique shops, and indulge in wine and fine-dining. Explore a musuem or winery, float down a lazy river, or simply kick back at one of the area's many bed and breakfasts or relaxing vacation rentals.

Gastehaus Schmidt is an excellent resource for finding some of the best in Texas Hill Country lodging.

[88] Marco Island Vacation Rentals from Horizon Rentals

Horizon Rentals offers premier Marco Island vacation rentals of all sizes and locations; from affordable to luxury, condo or home, beach to bay!

Marco Island, on Florida's peaceful southwest coast, is the perfect escape for those seeking the warmth and relaxation of a Florida beach resort without the hustle and bustle of some of the more crowded regions of this southern state. Sharing airport and interstate access with nearby Naples and Fort Myers, Marco Island is easily accessed, but much harder to leave.

Perfect for couples or families or groups of friends, Marco Island offers it all. Soak up the sun on some of the most beautiful beaches on the Gulf of Mexico. Explore the nearby everglades, charter a deep sea fishing vessel, or simply relax with a good book as the crimson sun sets on the shining horizon. Play a round of golf, followed by a couple matches of tennis, followed by fine dining or a casual meal with friends. The world is your oyster on Marco Island!

[86] Grandstay Suites—Perfect for Business Travellers

As Wisconsin's capital and second largest city, Madison is destination for all manor of visitors, both for work and for leisure. For those in town on business, for short or extended stays, Grandstay Residential Suites is your best option among Madison Wisconsin Hotels.

Grandstay specializes in catering to the needs of longer term guests in need of a home way from home during their time in Madison. Each studio or suite has unique decor, is fully furnished, and is equipped to meet each guest's daily needs. Fully functioning kitchens, large business desk, televisions, and phone and data lines all come standard.

Gourmet Express breakfasts each morning, swimming pool, whirl pool, exercise room, and backyard barbecue ensures that Grandstay guests enjoy their stay, always return, and might not want to leave.

[85] Hilton Head Rentals and Golf

Located on the warm coast of South Carolina is world renowned Hilton Head Island. The luxury escape is reputed as one of the finest golf and tennis destinations in North America. Dozens of championship courses, 12 miles of golden sand beaches, palm trees, warm Atlantic breezes, and sailboats on the horizon have made Hilton Head a playground for the high living.

One of the Island's nicest charms are the fabulous homes dotting the coast. These beach escapes are luxurious, but comfortable... just begging to be lounged to for a rejuvenating retreat from "the daily grind."

The Hilton Head rentals market is thriving. Large coastal homes and smaller villas are readily available for rental year round. These properties are an excellent option for a family reunion, family vacation, retreat for a group of friends, or an intimate escape with a partner.

[83] Caribbean Villa Escape

It will be truly difficult to find finer Caribbean vacation rentals than those offered by **Caribbean Villas and Resorts Management Co.**

For an ultra luxury villa on St. John or a selection of Tortola vacation rentals near white sand beaches, lush island jungles, and turquoise water, this is your first and best choice!

Picture yourself napping in a hammock under gently swaying palm trees, lounging in the hot tub with friends, reading a book by the pool, or playing billiards late into the night. This isn't just a vacation. It's a dream.

[82] Meetings on the Ocean—Myrtle Beach, SC

Not all travel is an escape from work. Unfortunately, for those offside meetings, conferences, and trainings, you are required to pack the office as well as your swimsuit and golf clubs. At least you're away from home and office. You get a change of routine and you're paid on top of it! That glass is definitely half full.

Now choosing a destination for that off-site meeting can be tricky. You must consider expense, weather, lodging and meeting accommodations, and whether the region offers enough entertainment options on the side.

Myrtle Beach, South Carolina happens to be a great compromise. Offering a mild climate, exceptional golfing, beaches, nightlife, restaurants, and affordable lodging, the city of Myrtle Beach is a great choice for a corporate escape.

[81] Golf Gulf Shores, Alabama

Located on Alabama's white sand gulf coast is the popular vacation destination of Gulf Shores. Extraordinary sunrises and sunset, a mild climate, and warm souther breezes make Gulf Shores an excellent winter retreat and is especially popular with the Northern Mid-Western states who suffer through extra long winter chills.

Among the many leisure vacation activities in the area, golfing is among the best in the country. The region features more than 288 holes to play, and the skill level varies from expert to beginner and everything in between. Among these many courses are also a selection designed by some of golf's biggest names, including:

Arnold Palmer, Larry Nelson, Bruce Devlin, Jerry Pate, Robert Von Hagge and Earl Stone.

[80] The Glidden House Tour De Circle

The Glidden House Inn of Ohio is a beautiful mansion renovated into a charming Cleveland Bed and Breakfast Hotel. Located near the Glidden House are a number of fine institutions for learning. For the benefit of its guests, the Inn has partnered with a select few of these institutions to offer an exciting Ohio vacation package: The *"Tour De Circle."*

The package includes overnight accommodations for two in a finely appointed guestroom, as well as admission to each of the following cultural centres:

- Museum of Natural History.
- Museum of Art.
- Western Reserve Historical Society.
- Botanical Gardens and Glass House.

Start off the evening by relaxing in your room, then begin your tour of discover through art exhibitions, natural wonders, and historic artifacts. In the morning you can sleep in or enjoy a complimentary lite breakfast.

[79] Squidoo Vacation Accommodations

Squidoo is one of the new social media outlets that has taken hold and risen above the ranks across the Internet. Its highly adaptable and flexible features makes it possible for users to create lenses (web pages) for an endless number of categories (travel and hospitality included).

For gathering related lenses, users can also create groups for their's and other's lenses. Vacation Accommodations and Ski Town Vacation Rentals are two new handy groups appropriate to the travel industry.

Categories

- Beach Vacation.
- Blogroll.
- Business Destinations.
- Destination Weddings.
- Destinations.
- Family Vacation.
- Golf Vacation.
- Miscellaneous.
- Mountain Getaways.
- Romantic Getaways.
- Ski Vacation.
- Urban Vacations.

Bibliography

Accounting Standards Committee of Germany, drsc.de.

Accounting Standards Review Board (New Zealand), asrb.co.nz.

Association of Accounting Technicians, aat.org.uk.

BUREZ Jonathan, VAN DEN POEL Dirk (2009), Separating Financial From Commercial Customer Churn: A Modeling Step Towards Resolving. The Conflict Between The Sales and Credit Department, Expert Systems with Applications, Forthcoming.. www.ugent.be. Retrieved on 2007-09-04.

Career: Sales Managers. iseek.org. Retrieved on 2007-07-09.

Cheryl Verstrate, *Homestay 101 for Hosts* (Start and Run a Successful Homestay), 1st edition, 2006.

Compendium of Professional Selling. United Professional Sales Association.

CPA Australia, cpaustralia.com.au.

Davis, Sid (2005). *A Survival Guide for Selling a Home*. AMACOM/ American Management Association, 4.

Financial Accounting, (2006). 12th, Boston, Mass: McGraw-Hill/Irwin, 261-263.

German Auditor Oversight Commission, apak-aoc.de.

German CPA Society, cgpas.de.

German Federal Financial Supervisory Authority (BaFin), bafin.de.

German Institute of Certified Public Accountants (IDW), idw.de.

Greening, Jack (1993). *Selling Without Confrontation*. The Haworth Press, Inc., 23.

http://dictionary.reference.com/browse/accountancy , dictionary.com

http://en.wikipedia.org/wiki/Hotel_manager

http://www.ifac.org/IAASB International Auditing and Assurance Standards Board (ifac.org.)

Jan Stankus, *How to Open and Operate a Bed and Breakfast* (Globe Pequot Press, 7th edition 2003).

Martha Watson Murphy and Amelia Rockwell Seton, *How to Start and Operate Your Own Bed-and-Breakfast/Down-to-Earth Advice from an Award-Winning B&B Owner* (Owlet, 1994).

Mary Davis, *So-you Want to be an Innkeeper: The Definitive Guide to Operating a Successful Bed-and-Breakfast or Country Inn* (Chronicle Books, 1996).

Matt. 25 : 19.

Malaysian Accounting Standards Board, masb.org.my.

Meigs and Meigs, *Financial Accounting,* Fourth Edition McGraw-Hill, 1983. p. 124.

Meigs, Walter B. and Robert F. Meigs. *Financial Accounting,* 4th ed. McGraw-Hill, 1970, p.1.

Monthly Wholesale Trade Survey Definitions Statements Retrieved from http://en.wikipedia.org/wiki/sales-(accounting).

OEC Tunisie, oect.org.tn.

Pinson, Linda and Jerry Jinnett. *Keeping the Books,* Second Edition Upstart Publishing Company, Inc., 1993. p. 15. This is a simplified example.

Quran 2: 282.

Random House Dictionary, Revised Edition, 1975.

Rumbauskas, Frank (2006). *Never Cold Call Again,* John Wiley & Sons, 192.

Sakach, Deborah Edwards, *Bed and Breakfasts and Country Inns* (American Historic Inns, Inc., 16th edition, 2004).

Sales.dictionary.com. Retrieved on 2007-04-07.

Sandee Wright, Owner and Innkeeper of Timberwolf Creek, Maggie Valley NC, Founder of CAIK (Caucus of American InnKeepers).

Securities and Exchange Board of India—Mail.

StreetAuthority: RevPAR defined:

Smith Travel Research: Global RevPAR data with a focus on the US.

Hotel Benchmark: Global RevPAR data with a focus on the UK.

The Bench: Global RevPAR data with a focus on daily data.

PKF Consulting: RevPAR data for select US cities.

MKG Consulting RevPAR data for Europe with a focus on France.

TRI Consulting RevPAR data for Europe with a focus on the UK.

Fairmas RevPAR data with a focus on Germany.

Susannah Craig and Park Davis, Complete Idiot's Guide to Running a Bed and Breakfast (Alpha Books, 2001).

Links

Agritourism.

Bcanada.com Bed and Breakfast Accommodation B&Bs.

BOnline.com.

Bedandbreakfast.com Worldwide Bed and Breakfasts Inns Directory.

Blue and White Motel in Montana.

Central City SRO Collaborative—a Non-profit in San Francisco that organizes and assists SRO tenants.

CouchSurfing.

Cozyplaces.com Your Premier Bed and Breakfast Directory.

GlobalFreeLoaders.

Homeshare International [2], charity organisation providing exchange of housing for help in the home.

Hospitality Club—currently the largest community.

http://dictionary.reference.com/browse/accountancy , dictionary.com

http://en.wikipedia.org/wiki/Accountancy

http://en.wikipedia.org/wiki/Bed_and_breakfast

http://en.wikipedia.org/wiki/Hospitality_service

http://en.wikipedia.org/wiki/Hotel_manager

http://www.ifac.org/IAASB International Auditing and Assurance Standards Board (ifac.org.).

Ibbp.com Bed and Breakfast Inn Travel directory.

LGHEI—Lesbian and Gay Hospitality Exchange International.

Motel Americana—a page devoted to history, narratives, and design of postwar motels.

Motel Signs—A collection of motel signs from around the US "America's Patel Motels".

Pamela Lanier's Bed and Breakfast Guide.

Pasporta Servo—for Esperanto speakers.

Pillows and Pancakes a B&B guide.

Selections New Zealand Bed and Breakfast Guide.

Servas International—human rights and global peace oriented.

Single Room Occupancy Hotels in Chicago.

TravelHoo [1]—a smaller international service.

WWOOF—"Worldwide opportunities on organic farms", a service demanding the traveller's help on the host's farm.

Index